MUSIC GAME of the WEEK

A year's worth of reproducible activities for the classroom or home

Brenda Knowis

Editor and fact-sheet author: Kris Kropff
Cover and book design: Brenda Knowis

©2008 Heritage Music Press,
a division of The Lorenz Corporation, and its licensors.
All rights reserved.

Printed in the United States of America

ISBN: 978-0-89328-859-4

Permission-to-Reproduce Notice

Permission to photocopy the student activities in this product is hereby granted to one teacher as part of the purchase price. This permission may only be used to provide copies for this teacher's specific classroom setting. This permission may not be transferred, sold, or given to any additional or subsequent user of this product. Thank you for respecting the copyright laws.

HERITAGE MUSIC PRESS
Diverse Resources for *Your* Music Classroom
a Lorenz company • www.lorenz.com

Foreword

This creative collection of puzzles, worksheets and activities is organized chronologically by holiday. We start the year with Secret Pal Day on January 12th and go clear through to Christmas and Hanukkah, stopping in between to celebrate the 100th Day of School, Earth Day, National Ice Cream Day, Take a Hike Day, and dozens more in between.

Offered at a variety of levels and addressing instrument and composer facts, terms and symbols, and note- and rhythm-reading, a topic index is provided on page 4 in case you want to use a particular activity at a non-seasonal time. (If we can have Christmas in July, why not Egg Day in February?!) Also provided is a reproducible composer fact sheet from which all of the composer questions in this resource have been taken.

Easy-to-follow directions are included, as are answers, and all pages are reproducible for single-classroom use. Great for Friday-afternoon fun or when a substitute teacher is in place. So what game is your class going to play this week?

—Brenda Knowis

Contents

GAME	HOLIDAY/SEASON	PAGE
Music Term Shuffle	Secret Pal Day	5
Popcorn Pop Quiz	National Popcorn Day	6
Did You Know?	Trivia Day	7
I Have a Dream	Martin Luther King Jr. Day	8
Birthday Sudoku	Mozart's Birthday	9
Solve Your Way to the 100th Day	100th Day	10
Pentatonic Phil	Groundhog Day	11
Happy Birthday, Handel!	Handel's Birthday	12
My Favorite Musician	Valentine's Day	13
Up, Down and All Around	Disaster Day	14
Shamrock Scramble	St. Patrick's Day	15
Word Wheel	Chopin's Birthday	16
Who's in the Basket?	Easter	17
Genius Sudoku	Einstein's Birthday	18
Foolin' or No Foolin'?	April Fool's Day	19
Earth Day Fast Facts	Earth Day	20
Upside-Down Dilemma	National Pineapple Upside-Down Day	21
Letter Tile Lingo	Humorous Day	22
All About Five	Cinco de Mayo	23
Mother's Day Maze	Mother's Day	24
Circus Celebration	Circus Day	25
Go Fly a Kite with Gershwin	Kite Day	26

GAME	HOLIDAY/SEASON	PAGE
Price It Right	Buy a Musical Instrument Day	27
High or Low?	Roller Coaster Anniversary	28
Instrument Scramble	Egg Day	29
Fishing with Dad	Father's Day	30
Juggling Jim	National Juggling Day	31
Word Wheel	Bicycle Patented	32
Flags and Fireworks	Independence Day	33
Birthday Sudoku	Mahler's Birthday	34
What's the Scoop?	National Ice Cream Day	35
Brain Busters	Puzzle Day	36
Code Breaker	First Fingerprint Taken	37
Music Style Shuffle	Relaxation Day	38
Back to School	Back to School	39
Up, Down and All Around	Roller Coaster Day	40
Know Your Notes Pumpkin Puzzler	First Day of Autumn	41
It's Up…It's Good	Football Season	42
No Work, Just Play for Labor Day	Labor Day	43
Hispanic Music and Musicians Word Search	National Hispanic Heritage Month	44
Spot the Difference	Make a Difference Day	45
Trick or Treat?	Halloween	46
Style Search	Sweetest Day	47
Define to Find	Dictionary Day	48
A Very Verdi Day	Verdi's Birthday	49
Take a Hike	Take a Hike Day	50
Let's Talk Turkey	Thanksgiving	51
Brain Busters	Use Less Stuff Day	52
Sandwich Stacker	National Sandwich Day	53
Trim the Tree	Christmas	54
Cookie Count	National Cookie Day	55
Music Note Dreidel	Hanukkah	56
What's the Word?	First Crossword Puzzle	57

Composer Fact Sheets 58

Answer Keys 61

Topic Index

Instruments and Ensembles
Solve Your Way to the 100th Day 10
Foolin' or No Foolin'? 19
Circus Celebration 25
High or Low? 28
Instrument Scramble 29
Fishing with Dad 30
Juggling Jim 31
Flags and Fireworks 33
Brain Busters 36
Back to School 39
Trick or Treat? 46
Let's Talk Turkey 51

Rhythm Reading and Notespellers
I Have a Dream 8
Pentatonic Phil 11
Earth Day Fast Facts 20
All About Five 23
What's the Scoop? 35
No Work, Just Play for Labor Day 43
Sandwich Stacker 55
Cookie Count 55

Terms and Symbols
Music Term Shuffle 5
Up, Down and All Around 14
Upside-Down Dilemma 21
Mother's Day Maze 24
Know Your Notes Pumpkin Puzzler 41
Take a Hike 49
Trim the Tree 54
Music Note Dreidel 56
What's the Word? 57

Composer, Performers, Works and Styles
Popcorn Pop Quiz 6
Birthday Sudoku 9
Happy Birthday, Handel! 12
My Favorite Musician 13
Word Wheel 16
Who's in the Basket? 17
Genius Sudoku 18
Letter Tile Lingo 22
Go Fly a Kite with Gershwin 26
Word Wheel 32
Birthday Sudoku 34
Code Breaker 37
Music Style Shuffle 38
Up, Down and All Around 40
It's Up…It's Good 42
Style Search 47
Define to Find 48
A Very Verdi Day 51

Various
Did You Know? 7
Hispanic Music and Musicians 44
Brain Busters 52

Cross-curricular
Shamrock Scramble 15
Earth Day Fast Facts 20
Price It Right 27
No Work, Just Play for Labor Day 43
Spot the Difference 45
Define to Find 48
A Very Verdi Day 49

Name _____ Date _____ Teacher _____

Music Term Shuffle

January • Secret Pal Day

Our Secret Pals are passing notes to answer the secret composer clue at the bottom of the page. But because they want to keep it a secret, they've jumbled all the words. To learn their secret, start by rearranging each group of letters to reveal a music term. Then, take all of the circled letters and shuffle them to find the secret composer.

1. TOPERS = __ __Ⓞ__ __ __

2. AMATERF = __ __ __ __ __ __Ⓞ

3. CATNCE = __ __ __ __Ⓞ__

4. TANDANE = __ __Ⓞ__ __ __

5. ROADMOTE = __ __ __ __ __ __ __ __

6. GALLORE = __Ⓞ__ __ __ __ __

7. TROFE = __ __ __ __ __

8. SYNCAMDI = __ __ __ __ __ __ __ __

9. YELDOM = __ __ __ __ __ __

10. SHARPE = __ __Ⓞ__ __ __

Scratch Pad

Shuffle the circled letters from above to answer the secret composer clue below.

My masterpiece was *Messiah*. ___ ___ ___ ___ ___ ___ ___

Name _____ Date _____ Teacher _____

Popcorn Pop Quiz

January • National Popcorn Day

January is bursting with yummy fun! Why? Because the 19th is National Popcorn Day. (I don't know about you, but I like mine with lots of butter or even caramel with peanuts.) To show our spirit for this popping day, we are having a Popcorn Pop Quiz. Here's how to play:

1. First, read the names in all of the popcorn kernels. Each one is a band or musician from the past or present.

2. Next, read the music styles on the four buckets at the bottom of the page.

3. Now, draw a line from each popcorn kernel to the music style most associated with that performer. When you are finished, count how many kernels are in each bucket and write the total on the line on each bucket.

© 2008 Heritage Music Press, a Lorenz company. All rights reserved.
This page may be reproduced for single-classroom use. This is a non-transferable license.

Name _____ Date _____ Teacher _____

Did you know?

January • Trivia Day

Music history is full of great bits of trivia—interesting facts and stories that are just fun to know. To mark Trivia Day, we thought we'd share a few with you. As you read each, match the fact to the composer, piece or instrument it describes by writing the correct letter in the space provided.

_____ 1. Most of the great masters of classical music wrote operas, but not this very famous German, late Romantic composer.

_____ 2. This ballet by Igor Stravinsky was premiered in Paris, France on May 29, 1913. To say that the audience didn't enjoy it is an understatement—they disliked it so much they shouted at the performers and eventually rioted!

_____ 3. Handel wrote this piece at the request of King George I, who wanted it for a very important celebration in a London park. But the premiere didn't go so well—it rained and there was an accident that caught some of the scenery on fire. (Don't worry, no one was hurt.)

_____ 4. This French, early Baroque composer was conducting one of his operas by pounding a large, heavy staff against the floor. Unfortunately, he missed the floor and struck his foot. The wound got infected with gangrene and he died a few weeks later.

_____ 5. The inventor of this woodwind instrument named it after himself.

_____ 6. Once, to create a piece of music, this 20th-century, American composer put a piece of paper outside in the rain. After a few drops fell on it, he took the paper inside and drew large staff lines on it so the raindrops became the notes. (Composing in this way, where elements of the music are determined by random, non-music things, like the roll of dice or the rain, is called *chance operations*.)

_____ 7. Early versions of this brass instrument didn't have valves. In order to change pitches, players had to pull out one section of the instrument and replace it with another tube of a different length. Called *crooks*, players rested as many as five of these sections over their arms when playing.

_____ 8. This composer nearly bankrupted a country! Here's the deal: King Ludwig of Bavaria really admired this composer's operas, so when he shared with the king his vision for a huge theater big enough for all the stage effects he had in mind for his four-opera cycle, *Der Ring des Nibelungen*, the king agreed to build such a theater in the city of Bayreuth. Well, this was a big theater and it cost a lot of money. Finally, others in the Bavaria government had to step in before King Ludwig gave away all the country's money. (Another interesting bit of trivia: King Ludwig also had Neuschwanstein built. This is the castle after which Cinderella's castle at Disneyworld is modeled.)

_____ 9. This orchestral piece written by French composer Hector Berlioz in 1830 used one of the largest orchestras of the day. It included more than 85 musicians, including 4 bassoonists (2 were typical), 3 tuba players (most orchestras had just 1) and 4 harpists (again, 1 was the norm).

_____ 10. This Italian Renaissance composer was one of the first to write dynamics in his music.

A.	Johannes Brahms	F.	*Music for the Royal Fireworks*
B.	John Cage	G.	*The Rite of Spring*
C.	Giovanni Gabrieli	H.	Saxophone
D.	Horn	I.	*Symphonie fantastique*
E.	Jean-Baptiste Lully	J.	Richard Wagner

© 2008 Heritage Music Press, a Lorenz company. All rights reserved.
This page may be reproduced for single-classroom use. This is a non-transferable license.

Name _____ Date _____ Teacher _____

I Have a Dream

January • Martin Luther King Day

Name each of the notes below to complete these facts about Martin Luther King, Jr. and his "I Have a Dream" speech.

1. King gave his famous S P____ ____ ____ H on August 28, 1963.

2. His speech was delivered to over 200,000 civil rights supporters, and is considered to

be one of the greatest and most N O T____ ____ L ____ speeches in history.

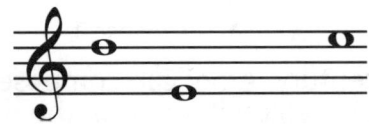

3. The speech was ____ ____ L I V ____ R E D from the steps of the Lincoln Memorial.

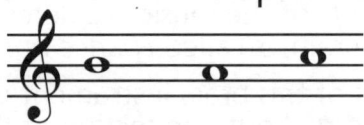

4. King spoke of his desire for a future where ____ L ____ ____ K S and whites would coexist as equals.

5. Due to King's speech and march, he was N ____ M ____ ____ Man of the Year by TIME magazine for 1963, and in 1964, he was the youngest person ever awarded the Nobel Peace Prize.

6. Early in his speech he refers to Lincoln's Gettysburg ____ D ____ R ____ S S, saying, in part, "Five score years ago..."

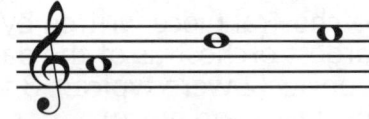

7. Famous excerpt: "I have a dream that my four little ____ H I L ____ R ____ N will one day live in a nation where they will not be judged by the color of their skin but by the content of their character."

Name _____ Date _____ Teacher _____

Birthday Sudoku

January • Mozart's Birthday

Wolfgang Amadeus Mozart was born on January 27, 1756. To solve these Birthday Sudoku puzzles, you need to put one—and only one—of each of the letters from Mozart's name in:
- each row
- each column
- each 2x3 box that's within the bigger grid

These are the same rules as "regular" number sudoku, but in this puzzle, you'll use:

M O Z A R T

M					T
	A	R			
			O	Z	
		T		A	
A			Z		
	Z				R

A				M	
		M	A		
O	T			A	R
A	M			Z	T
			A	T	
		R			O

© 2008 Heritage Music Press, a Lorenz company. All rights reserved.
This page may be reproduced for single-classroom use. This is a non-transferable license.

Name _____ Date _____ Teacher _____

Solve your way to the 100th Day

February • 100th Day

Congratulations! You've made it through 100 days! Your job is to find your way through the 100-box maze below by coloring in just the squares that contain percussion instruments.

Have fun celebrating the number 100!

Begin Here	Ukulele	Flute	String Bass	Banjo	Accordian	Saxophone	Banjo	Trombone	Piano
Tambourine	Timpani	Trumpet	Accordian	Violin	Rainstick	Maracas	Handbells	String Bass	Bassoon
String Bass	Guiro	Triangle	Harp	Clarinet	Tom-Tom	Trombone	Castanets	Piccolo Trumpet	Piccolo
Piano	Trombone	Snare Drum	Flugelhorn	Tuba	Cymbals	F Horn	Metallophone	Guitar	Trombone
Tuba	Oboe	Glockenspiel	F Horn	Oboe	Claves	Viola	Bongos	Bassoon	Dulcimer
Violin	Saxophone	Snare Drum	Conga Drum	Xylophone	Drum Set	Recorder	Bass Drum	Djembe	Tuba
Piano	Piccolo Trumpet	Clarinet	Tuba	Viola	Flute	Trumpet	Cello	Chimes	Piano
Alto Sax	String Bass	Fife	Trumpet	Synthesizer	Cello	Tuba	Vibraphone	Timbales	Flugelhorn
Trumpet	Pan Flute	Harmonica	Guitar	F Horn	Accordian	Flute	Gong	Guitar	F Horn
Harp	Mandolin	Piccolo	Trumpet	Viola	Ukulele	Violin	Log Drum	Cabasa	End Here

© 2008 Heritage Music Press, a Lorenz company. All rights reserved.
This page may be reproduced for single-classroom use. This is a non-transferable license.

Name _____ Date _____ Teacher _____

Pentatonic Phil

February • Groundhog Day

This Groundhog Day, when Pentatonic Phil comes out of his hole, he isn't looking for his shadow, he is looking for time signatures. Read each music example below, then circle its time signature. Be sure you choose correctly, or we'll have six more weeks of winter!

A. 4/4   3/4   ♩ ♪ ♩ | ♩. ♩ ||

B. 4/4   3/4   ♩ ♩ | ♩ ♪ ♩ ||

C. 4/4   2/4   ♩ ♩ ♩ | — ♪ ♪ ||

D. 6/8   2/4   ♫ ♩ | ♩ ♩ ||

E. 6/8   2/4   ♩. ♩. | ♫♫ ♩. ||

F. 4/4   2/4   ♫♪ ♪ | ♫♫ ♩. ||

G. 3/4   4/4   o | | - ||

H. 2/4   3/4   ♫♫ ♪ | ♫ ♪ ♫ ||

I. 6/8   3/4   ♪ ♫ ♪ ♫ | ♫ ♩ ♪ ||

J. 6/8   2/4   ♪♪ ♪ ♫ ♫ ||

K. 4/4   6/8   ♩ ♫♫ ♩ | ♩ ♩ ||

L. 4/4   3/4   ♪ ♫ ♪ | ♪ ♩ ♪ ||

© 2008 Heritage Music Press, a Lorenz company. All rights reserved.
This page may be reproduced for single-classroom use. This is a non-transferable license.

Name _____ Date _____ Teacher _____

Happy Birthday, Handel!

February • Handel's Birthday

February 23rd is Handel's birthday. Answer the questions below to solve this crossword puzzle all about the birthday boy.

Across

1. During what period did Handel compose?
4. Handel's first musical love was what?
6. Where is Handel buried?
7. To what country did Handel move when he was 25? (Hint: He lived there for the rest of his life.)

Down

2. Oratorios are extended choral works that tell what kind of stories?
3. Where was Handel born?
5. What is the title of Handel's most famous oratorio?

© 2008 Heritage Music Press, a Lorenz company. All rights reserved.
This page may be reproduced for single-classroom use. This is a non-transferable license.

Name _____ Date _____ Teacher _____

My Favorite Musician

February • Valentine's Day

Show some love for your favorite musician or band by creating a Valentine Basket in their honor! You'll need:

- A piece of 11x17" paper
- A 1x17" strip of paper
- Markers, crayons or colored pencils
- Scissors
- Glue stick
- Old magazines that you're allowed to cut apart (opt.)

Steps (see illustrations below):

1. Cut a piece of 11x17" paper in half, long ways, to create two strips that are each 5 1/2x17". Fold each piece in half widthwise.
2. Lay one piece on top of the other so they line up exactly and round off the corners of the **open end** with scissors.
3. Open the two pieces and lay them on your desk, one on top of the other, so they form an X. Fold up the lower half of the bottom strip, place a little glue on the strip you just folded, then fold up the lower half on the top piece. Turn over your basket and glue those sides together. Be careful not to glue your basket closed.
4. Take the 1x17" strip and write your name on one side. Then, attach it to your basket as shown below to create a handle for your basket. (Be sure to attach it name-side down.) Now your basket is ready to decorate!
5. First, think about your favorite musician or band. But just think, you want to keep it a secret. Now, write facts about this person or group on your basket. Then, color it with crayons or markers, or glue on words or pictures you cut out of magazines.
6. When your basket is finished, display it in your classroom. Ask your classmates if they can guess your favorite musician. See if you can guess theirs.

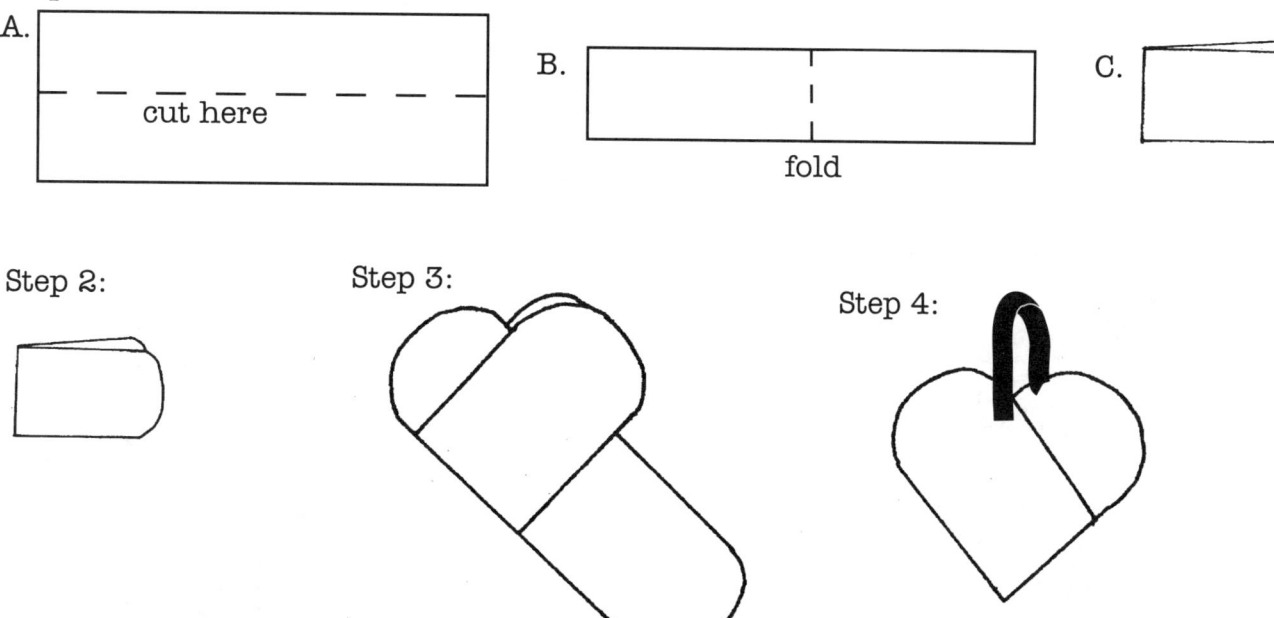

© 2008 Heritage Music Press, a Lorenz company. All rights reserved.
This page may be reproduced for single-classroom use. This is a non-transferable license.

Name _____ Date _____ Teacher _____

Up, Down and All Around

February • Disaster Day

A big storm came through and mixed up all of our music vocabulary words. Help our town with the clean up by finding the 17 music terms hidden in this grid. The terms are in order as they appear below and they follow each other and zigzag in a snake-like pattern through the grid. Once you discover the first music term, you should be able to find the other 16. There are no extra letters and the words can be forwards or backwards. Try highlighting the words as you discover them and watch the snake take shape.

Begin here and continue down each column.	Eighth Note	Scale	Melody	Allegro
	Legato	Rhythm	Chord	Fermata
	Accent	Harmony	Phrase	
	Sharp	Duet	Pitch	
	Clef	Octave	Tempo	

C	E	N	T	S	H	A	R	P	C
C	R	E	L	A	C	S	F	E	L
A	H	O	F	E	R	M	A	T	A
O	Y	R	G	E	L	L	A	O	P
T	T	P	I	T	C	H	T	E	M
A	H	E	S	A	R	H	P	D	R
G	M	E	L	O	D	Y	C	H	O
E	H	M	E	V	A	T	C	O	T
L	A	R	M	O	N	Y	D	U	E
E	T	O	N	H	T	H	G	I	E

© 2008 Heritage Music Press, a Lorenz company. All rights reserved.
This page may be reproduced for single-classroom use. This is a non-transferable license.

14

Name _____ Date_____ Teacher_____

Shamrock Scramble

March • St. Patrick's Day

The 4 letters in the shamrock below spell an important word in music. In fact, without this, there wouldn't be much music. Do you know what it is or do you need a little luck of the Irish to solve it?

Music word: _____

Now that you've solved that, see how many more words you can create using these 4 letters. Give yourself 2 points for each two-letter word, 3 points for each three-letter word, 4 points for each four-letter word and 5 points for each five-letter word.

IMPORTANT: You may use each letter multiple times in the same word.

Total Points   = _____

Name _____ Date _____ Teacher _____

word Wheel

March • Composer Birthday

Did you know that March 1st is a famous composer's birthday? Discover who it is by putting the first letter of each picture clue in the inner ring of the circle.

_____, was born on March 1, 1810.

© 2008 Heritage Music Press, a Lorenz company. All rights reserved.
This page may be reproduced for single-classroom use. This is a non-transferable license.

Name _____ Date_____ Teacher_____

Who's in the Basket?

March • Easter

Read the clues below to discover which three composers are in your Easter basket. When you know who's who, write the composer's name on the corresponding egg in the basket.

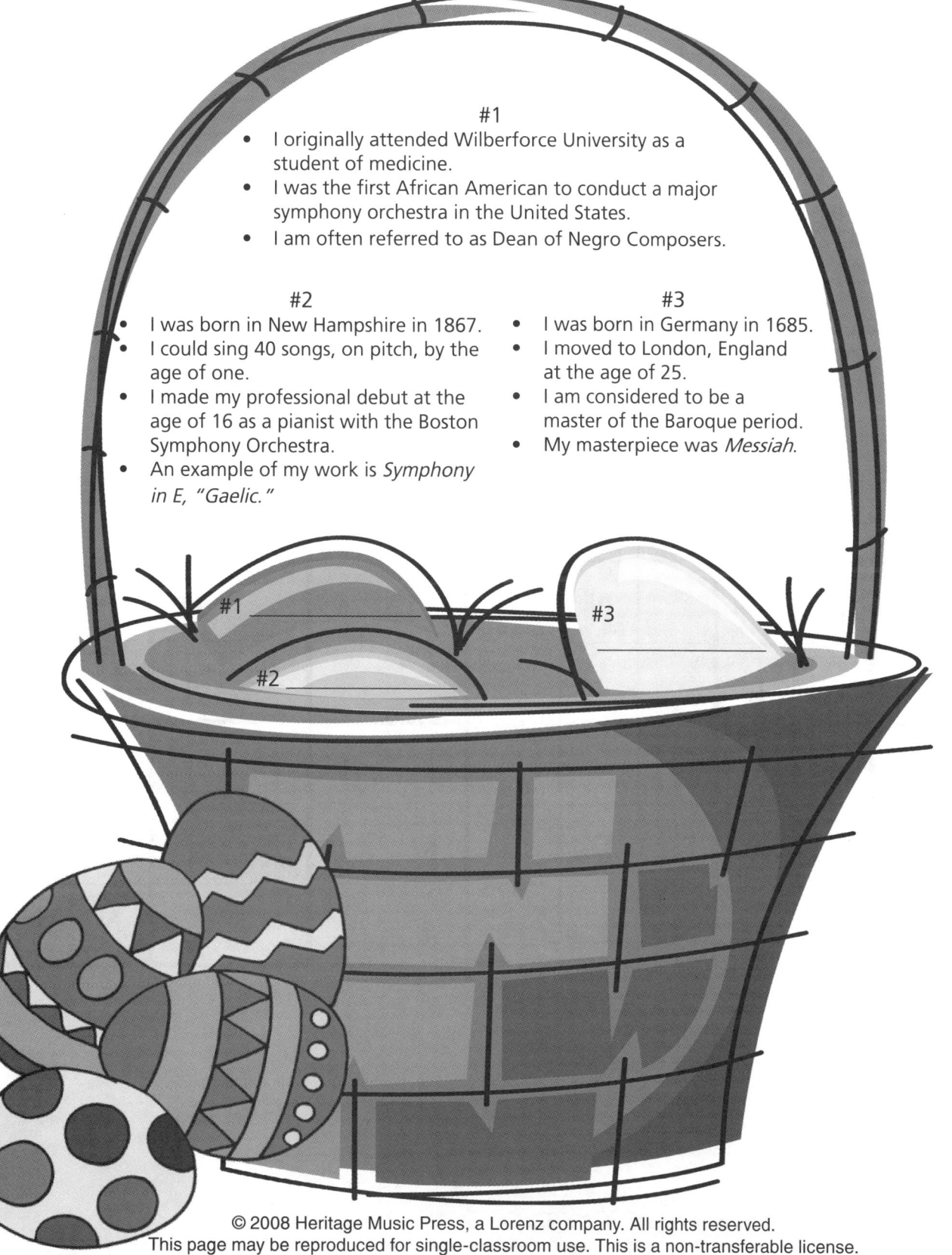

#1
- I originally attended Wilberforce University as a student of medicine.
- I was the first African American to conduct a major symphony orchestra in the United States.
- I am often referred to as Dean of Negro Composers.

#2
- I was born in New Hampshire in 1867.
- I could sing 40 songs, on pitch, by the age of one.
- I made my professional debut at the age of 16 as a pianist with the Boston Symphony Orchestra.
- An example of my work is *Symphony in E, "Gaelic."*

#3
- I was born in Germany in 1685.
- I moved to London, England at the age of 25.
- I am considered to be a master of the Baroque period.
- My masterpiece was *Messiah*.

#1 _____
#2 _____
#3 _____

© 2008 Heritage Music Press, a Lorenz company. All rights reserved.
This page may be reproduced for single-classroom use. This is a non-transferable license.

Name _____ Date _____ Teacher _____

Genius Sudoku

March • Einstein's Birthday

Albert Einstein was born on March 14, 1879. He was a genius of science. Can you think of some geniuses of music? Mozart? Yes. Bach? Definitely. Beethoven? For sure. Handel? Absolutely.

To solve these Genius Sudoku puzzle, you need to put one—and only one—of each of the letters from handel's name shown below in:
- each row
- each column
- each 2x3 box that's within the bigger grid

These are the same rules as "regular" number sudoku, but in this puzzle, you'll use:

H A N D E L

L				E	H
D		H			N
		N	L		
		E	A		
A			H		D
H	L			A	E

N	A	H			D
			D		A
			A	L	
		D	L		A
E			A		
A			E	N	H

© 2008 Heritage Music Press, a Lorenz company. All rights reserved.
This page may be reproduced for single-classroom use. This is a non-transferable license.

Name _____ Date _____ Teacher _____

Foolin' or No Foolin'?

April • April Fool's Day

Below are some facts about various musical instruments. Some are true and some are false. See if you can find all the facts we are foolin' about. Then fill in the appropriate circle beside each fact.

We'll give you a hint: there are 7 no foolin' facts (or are we foolin' you?).

Foolin' (false)   **No Foolin' (true)**

○ ○ 1. All four members of the violin family have five strings.

○ ○ 2. The five main members of the Woodwind Family are the flute, oboe, clarinet, saxophone, and bassoon.

○ ○ 3. Flutes are commonly used in jazz bands.

○ ○ 4. The mellophone is a member of the brass family.

○ ○ 5. The Percussion Family is the largest of all the instrument families.

○ ○ 6. A cello is larger than a violin and a string bass.

○ ○ 7. A guitar has 6 strings and can be either acoustic or electric.

○ ○ 8. A clarinet is a double-reed instrument.

○ ○ 9. A tambourine is a membranophone and is part of the Percussion Family.

○ ○ 10. All woodwind instruments use a reed to produce sound.

○ ○ 11. The string bass is usually played sitting down, with the instrument resting between the legs.

○ ○ 12. The trombone uses a slide to change pitch.

○ ○ 13. A snare drum, tom-toms, bass drum and cymbals are some of the instruments included in a drum set.

○ ○ 14. When you hear electric guitars, bass and drums mixed with steel pedal guitars, and often a fiddle, you're listening to Classical Music.

○ ○ 15. The saxophone is a member of the brass family.

© 2008 Heritage Music Press, a Lorenz company. All rights reserved.
This page may be reproduced for single-classroom use. This is a non-transferable license.

Name _____ Date _____ Teacher _____

Earth Day Fast Facts

April • Earth Day

Name each of the notes below to complete these fascinating facts about earth!

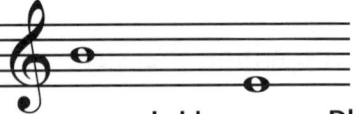

1. Earth is referred to as the ____ L U ____ Planet.

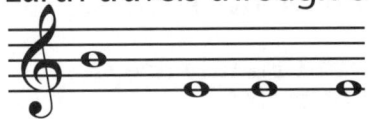

2. Earth travels through S P ____ ____ ____ at 66,700 miles per hour.

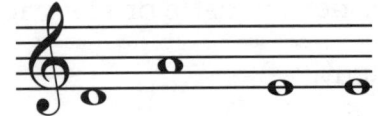

3. The ___ R ___ ___ Z ___ carries about 100 million tons of sand particles around earth yearly. That means if you visit a beach in America, you could have sand that came from the Gobi desert in China.

4. Earth's oceans are an average of 2 miles ___ ___ ___ P.

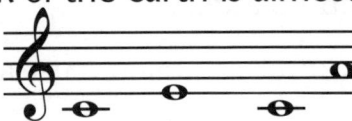

5. The ___ I ___ M ___ T ___ R of the earth is almost 8,000 miles.

6. Earth is made of the following ___ H ___ M I ___ ___ L elements:

- oxygen
- aluminum
- iron
- sodium
- magnesium
- calcium
- potassium
- silicon
- other

© 2008 Heritage Music Press, a Lorenz company. All rights reserved.
This page may be reproduced for single-classroom use. This is a non-transferable license.

Name _____ Date _____ Teacher _____

Upside-Down Dilemma
April • National Pineapple Upside-Down Day

The month of April is full of good things and one of them is a day dedicated to Pineapple Upside-Down Cake! How delightful! To follow with the theme, some of the music symbols below are upside-down. Do you know which ones? Circle each one you find. Next, write the name for each symbol in the space provided under each pineapple. Use the word bank if you need help.

Word Bank
fermata
natural
quarter rest
flat
treble clef
fortissimo
bass clef
eighth note

Name _____ Date _____ Teacher _____

Letter Tile Lingo

April • Humorous Day

April has a funny day. No, it's not April Fools Day. It is Humorous Day. We thought it would be fun to share some humorous music facts with you. To solve each puzzle. Unscramble the tiles to rebuild a section of the fact. You may want to cut the tiles out to help you arrange them in the correct order. A space on the tile indicates a space between words.

PUZZLE #1

When Paul McCartney from The Beatles married Linda Eastman in 1969, no other ....

_____

| BEAT | THE | ING | TTEN | DED | LE A | WEDD |

PUZZLE #2

Happy Birthday To You was written in the 1890s by schoolteacher Mildred Hall. The lyrics were originally...

_____

| MOR | GOOD | ALL | NING | TO |

PUZZLE #3

A fact you may not know about Eminem. He wanted to be a ...

_____

| OK A | RTIS | T | C BO | COMI |

PUZZLE #4

Ukulele means _____ _____ in Hawaiian, and refers to the fast movement of the player's fingers.

| PIN | LEA | G F | JUM |

PUZZLE #5

_____ _____ is named after the Australian opera singer Dame Nellie Melba (1861-1931).

| AST | MELB | A TO |

PUZZLE #6

At the age of two, Mozart identified a _____ _____ as the pitch of G#.

| EAL | SQU | 'S | PIG |

Name _____ Date _____ Teacher _____

All About Five

May • Cinco de Mayo

The holiday of Cinco de Mayo, which means "5th of May," honors the victory of the Mexican militia over the French army at The Battle of Puebla in 1862. It is not, as many people think, Mexico's Independence Day, which is actually September 16. To celebrate Cinco de Mayo, let's review rhythms. Look at the somreros around the page. Each one contains a rhythm. Circle the sombrero if the rhythm equals five beats.

© 2008 Heritage Music Press, a Lorenz company. All rights reserved.
This page may be reproduced for single-classroom use. This is a non-transferable license.

23

Name _____ Date _____ Teacher _____

Mother's Day Maze

May • Mother's Day

How many flowers did you pick for Mom? In the maze below, follow the path marked by the whole notes to help you get from start to finish. When you are done, count the number of whole notes you "picked" along the way and write that number in the blank at the bottom of the page.

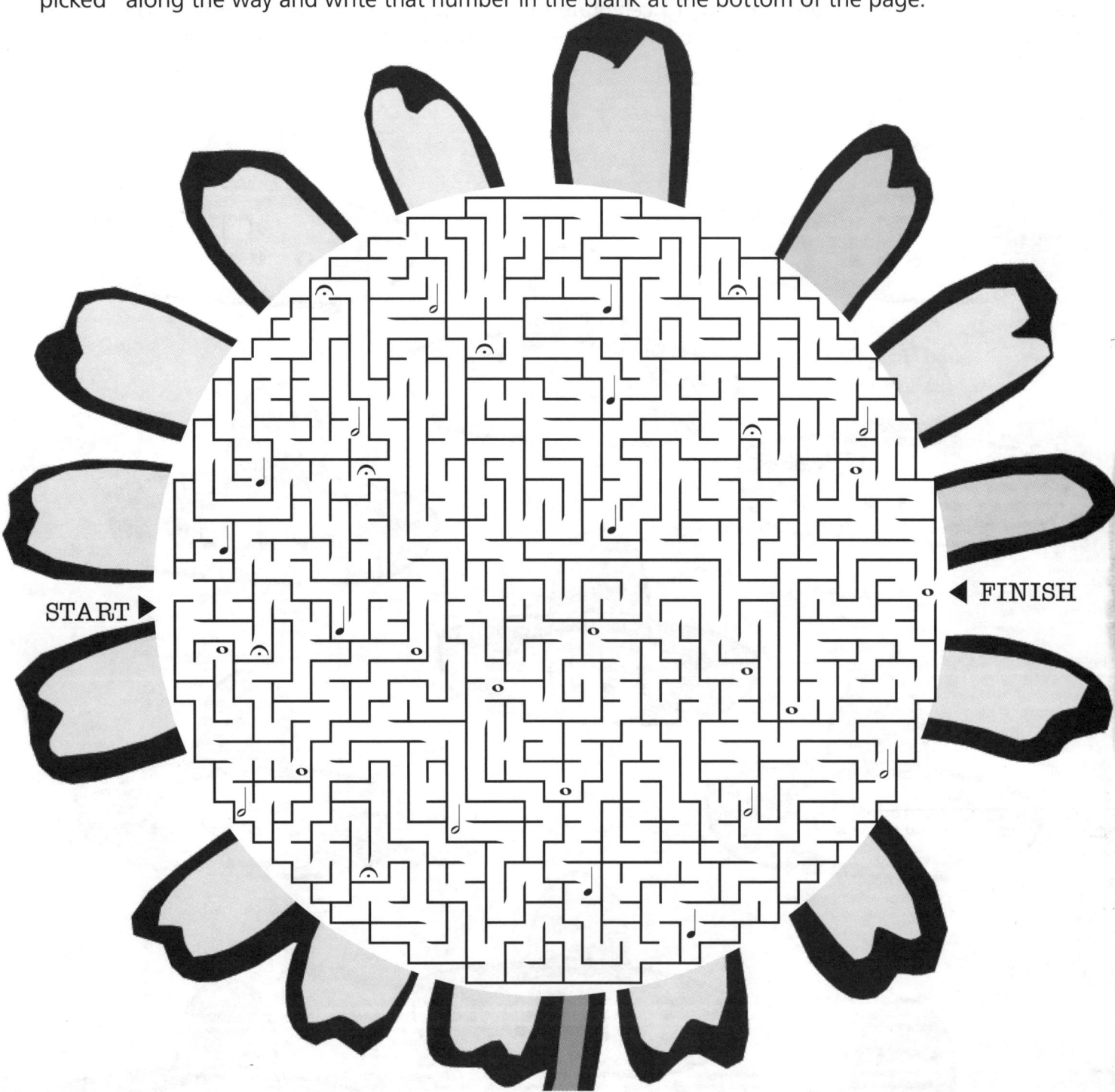

I picked _____ flowers for my Mom.

© 2008 Heritage Music Press, a Lorenz company. All rights reserved.
This page may be reproduced for single-classroom use. This is a non-transferable license.

Name _____ Date _____ Teacher _____

Circus Celebration

May • Circus Day

Do you like a circus? I sure do. Pictured below are lots of things you might find at the circus. Name them, and write the first letter of each picture clue in the blank below that picture. Together, they spell the name of an ensemble that you might hear at the circus. Rearrange the letters to reveal the answer. Do you know what it is?

___ ___ ___ ___

___ ___ ___ ___

 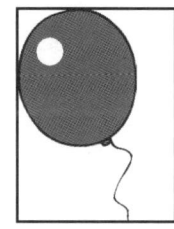  

___ ___ ___ ___

Name that band: _____ _____

© 2008 Heritage Music Press, a Lorenz company. All rights reserved.
This page may be reproduced for single-classroom use. This is a non-transferable license.

Name _____ Date _____ Teacher _____

Go Fly a Kite with Gershwin

May • Kite Day

May 12th is Kite Day. See if you can find all the famous composers flying around inside the kite below. The names can be straight across, up and down, diagonal, or even backwards.

RAVEL BERNSTEIN VIVALDI
COPLAND MOZART
HANDEL GRIEG
CHOPIN STRAUSS
BACH HAYDN
PURCELL
GERSHWIN
BIZET

JOPLIN
PUCCINI
SCHUBERT
TCHAIKOVSKY ROSSINI BARTÓK
BEETHOVEN BRAHMS
DEBUSSY
MENDELSSOHN

© 2008 Heritage Music Press, a Lorenz company. All rights reserved.
This page may be reproduced for single-classroom use. This is a non-transferable license.

Name _____ Date _____ Teacher _____

Price It Right

May • Buy a Musical Instrument Day

The month of May has a special day just for buying a musical instrument. To celebrate this awesome day, we are going instrument shopping. The store clerk has just finished pricing the instruments. Now you get to go shopping. There are several stacks of money to the right. Draw a line from the instrument to the correct stack of money.

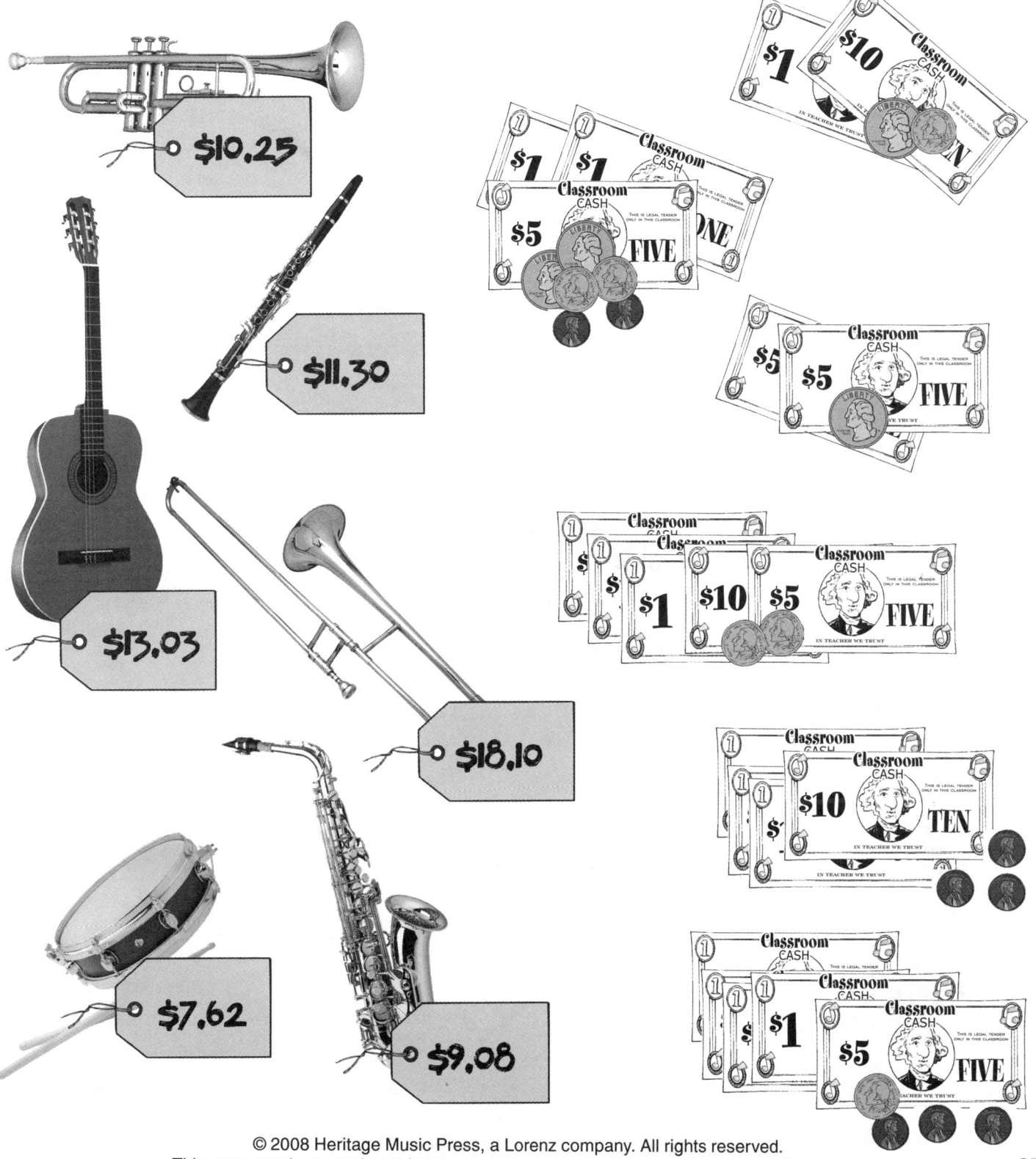

© 2008 Heritage Music Press, a Lorenz company. All rights reserved.
This page may be reproduced for single-classroom use. This is a non-transferable license.

Name _____ Date _____ Teacher _____

High or Low?

June • Roller Coaster Anniversary

On June 13, 1884, the first roller coaster opened in Coney Island, New York. I love roller coasters. Do you? You get highs and lows as you ride the track. Well, music has highs and lows too. Look at the pictures of the instruments below and decide if they make mostly high or low sounds. If it is high, mark it with an "H." If it is low, mark it with an "L."

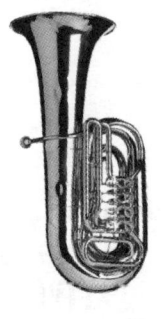         

_____   _____   _____   _____

_____   _____   _____

   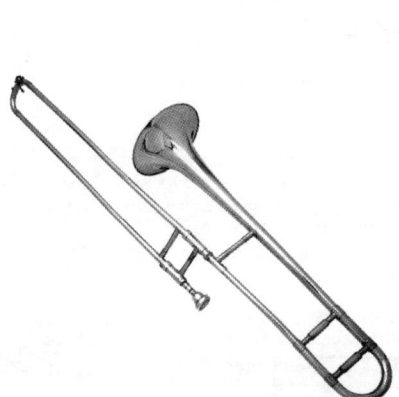   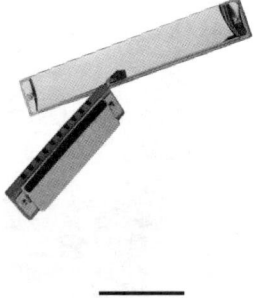   

_____   _____   _____   _____

© 2008 Heritage Music Press, a Lorenz company. All rights reserved.
This page may be reproduced for single-classroom use. This is a non-transferable license.

Name _____ Date _____ Teacher _____

Instrument Scramble

June • Egg Day

How do you like your eggs? I like mine scrambled with cheese. To celebrate Egg Day, we have scrambled the letters of several instrument names. See if you can unscramble the letters below to spell the name of the instrument. Once you've unscrambled each group of letters, draw a line from the instrument name to its picture.

charmaion

metputr

ragtiu

letganir

mrud

mateinboru

nebtromo

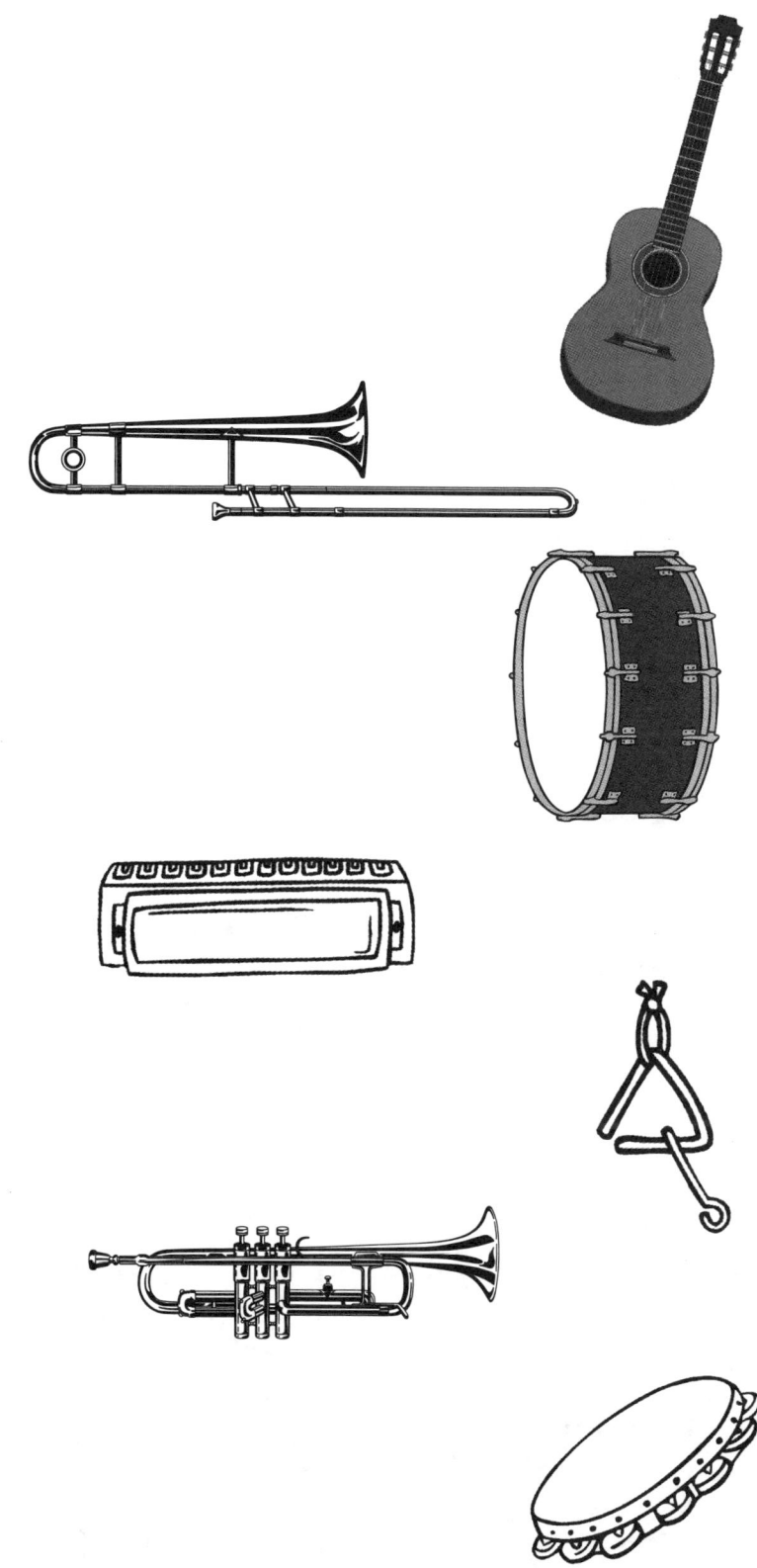

© 2008 Heritage Music Press, a Lorenz company. All rights reserved.
This page may be reproduced for single-classroom use. This is a non-transferable license.

29

Name _____ Date _____ Teacher _____

Fishing with Dad

June • Father's Day

Let's go fishing with Dad for Father's Day and see how many instruments we can catch. See if you can catch and color the instruments based on the family to which they belong. The instrument families are listed below, along with instructions for how to color each.

Color the Brass instruments blue.
Color the Percussion instruments red.
Color the String instruments yellow.
Color the Woodwind instruments green.

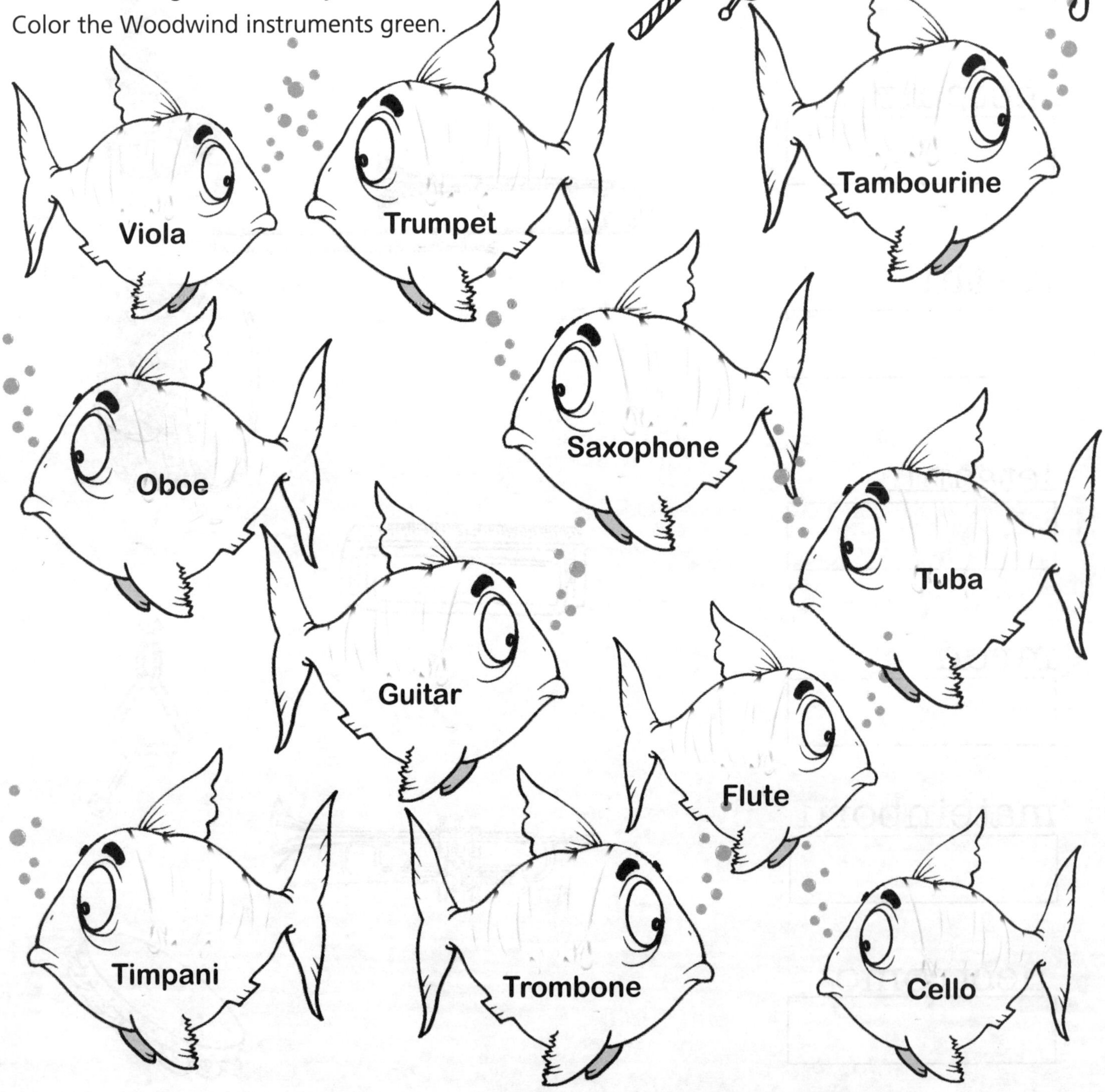

Viola
Trumpet
Tambourine
Oboe
Saxophone
Tuba
Guitar
Flute
Timpani
Trombone
Cello

© 2008 Heritage Music Press, a Lorenz company. All rights reserved.
This page may be reproduced for single-classroom use. This is a non-transferable license.

Name _____ Date _____ Teacher _____

Juggling Jim

June • National Juggling Day

Juggling Jim has jumbled all the instruments and cannot figure out which instrument belongs to which instrument family. Can you help him? Draw a line going from each instrument ball to the correct instrument family box.

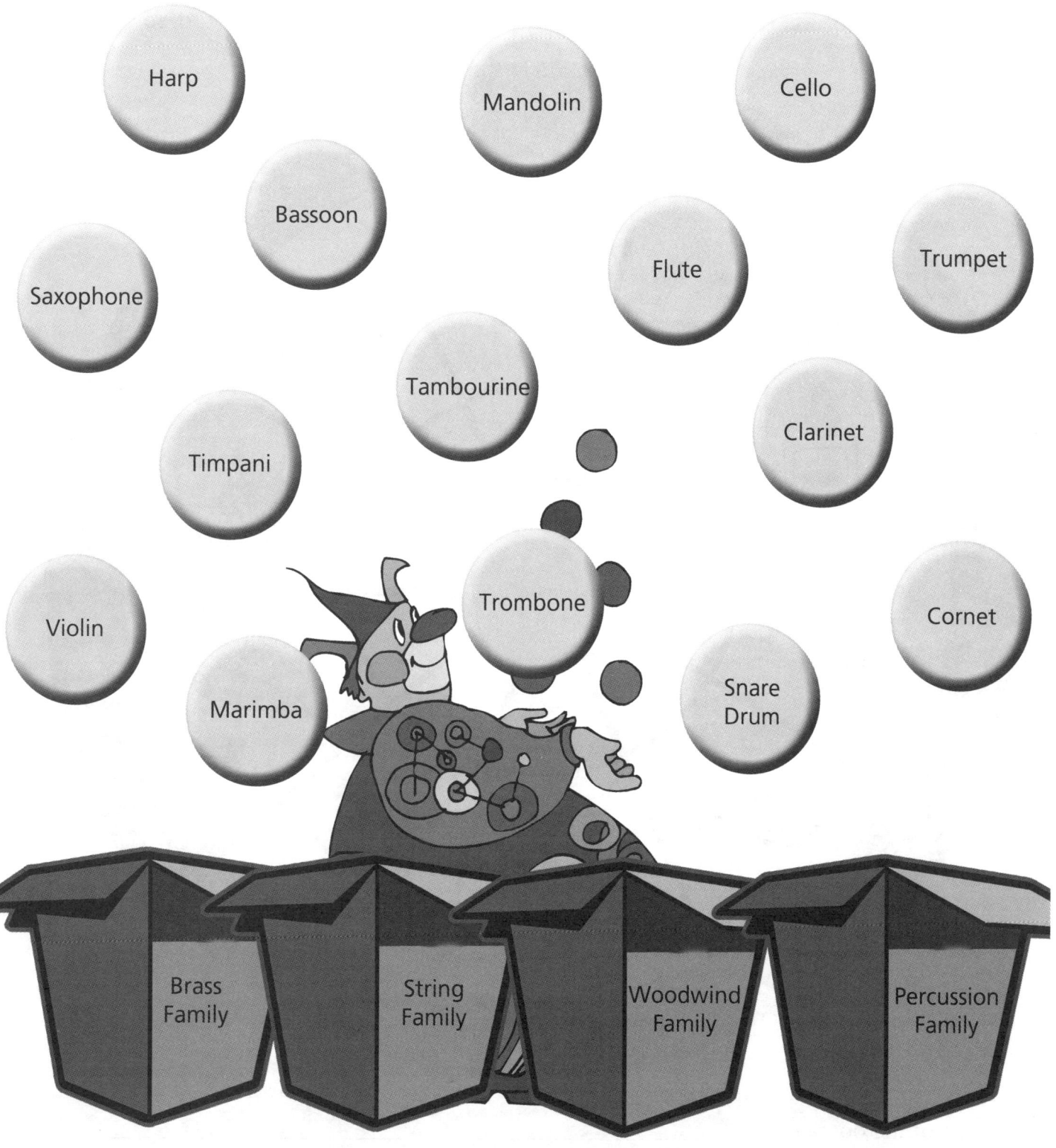

© 2008 Heritage Music Press, a Lorenz company. All rights reserved.
This page may be reproduced for single-classroom use. This is a non-transferable license.

Name _____ Date _____ Teacher _____

word wheel

June • Bicycle Patented

Did you know? The first bicycle, which was made in 1817 by Baron von Drais, didn't have any pedals. People walked it along! Even though the bicycle was patented two years later, on June 26, 1819, it took almost 50 years for pedals to be added so people could finally ride their bikes. To celebrate this invention, put the first letter of each picture in the bicycle wheel below to spell out the name of a famous opera by Mozart. You will have to decide where to start and stop each word, so put on that thinking cap.

The name of the opera is: The _____

© 2008 Heritage Music Press, a Lorenz company. All rights reserved.
This page may be reproduced for single-classroom use. This is a non-transferable license.

Name _____ Date _____ Teacher _____

Flags and Fireworks

July • Independence Day

It's the 4th of July and here comes the marching band in the parade. Circle all the instruments you would find in a marching band. Bonus activity: Write the name of each instrument next to its picture.

© 2008 Heritage Music Press, a Lorenz company. All rights reserved.
This page may be reproduced for single-classroom use. This is a non-transferable license.

Name _____ Date _____ Teacher _____

Birthday Sudoku

July • Composer Birthday

Gustav Mahler was born on July 7, 1860. To solve these Birthday Sudoku puzzles, you need to put one—and only one—of each of the letters from his name in the puzzle shown below in:
- each row
- each column
- each 2x3 box that's within the bigger grid

These are the same rules as "regular" number sudoku, but in this puzzle, you'll use the letters from his first name for the puzzle on the left and the letters from his last name for the puzzle on the right.

GUSTAV   MAHLER

	T			G	
U					S
	S	V			
		T	A		
T					A
	V			U	

	M	H		L	R
		L			M
		R			E
		A			H
		E			R
	R	M		A	H

34

© 2008 Heritage Music Press, a Lorenz company. All rights reserved.
This page may be reproduced for single-classroom use. This is a non-transferable license.

Name _____ Date _____ Teacher _____

What's the scoop?

July • National Ice Cream Day

Let's celebrate National Ice Cream Day by getting the scoop on note values! There's a note or rest in each of the ice cream cones below. Decide how many beats each one gets in 4/4 time and draw that number of scoops on top of the cone. Hurry before all the ice cream melts!

My favorite flavor of ice cream is _____.

© 2008 Heritage Music Press, a Lorenz company. All rights reserved.
This page may be reproduced for single-classroom use. This is a non-transferable license.

Name _____ Date _____ Teacher _____

Brain Busters

July • Puzzle Day

Brain Busters are picture puzzles illustrating music concepts. The answers to puzzles 1 and 2 are instrument names. Puzzles 3 and 4 are instrument classifications. Remember to think creatively as you look at the picture clues!

Puzzle #1

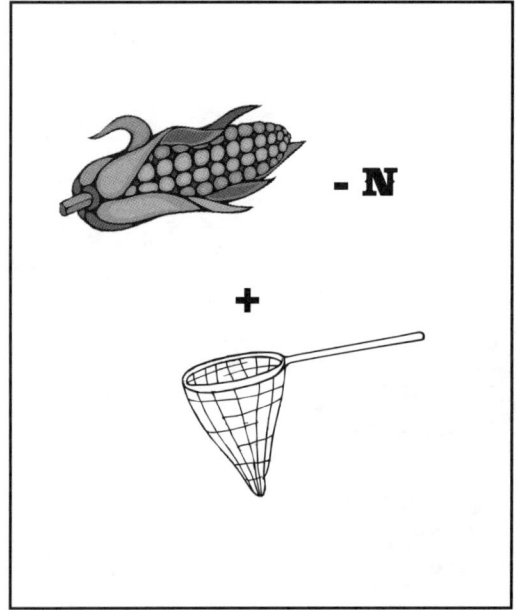

Answer: _____

Puzzle #2

Answer: _____

Puzzle #3

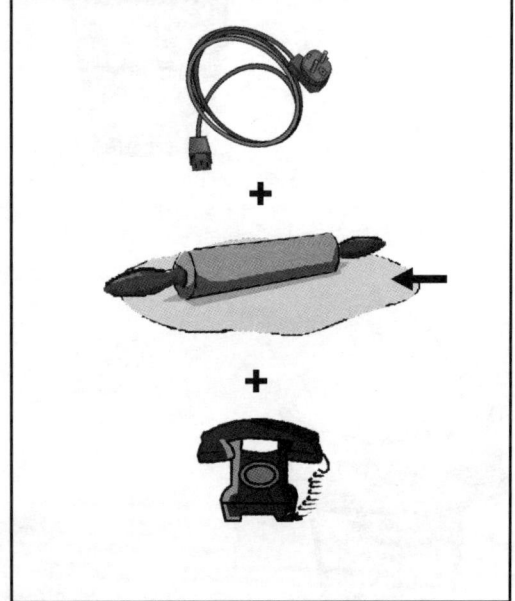

Answer: _____

Puzzle #4

Answer: _____

Name _____ Date _____ Teacher _____

Code Breaker

July • First Fingerprint Taken

Did you know that the first fingerprint was taken on July 28, 1858? Well, our Master Music Detective sure does, and he also knows other detective tricks, like writing his notes in code. Use the code key below to complete the fascinating facts our detective has collected about some very famous composers.

1	2	3	4	5	6	7	8	9	10	11	12	13
B	C	D	E	F	G	H	I	J	K	L	M	N

14	15	16	17	18	19	20	21	22	23	24	25	26
O	P	Q	R	S	T	U	V	W	X	Y	Z	A

1. Beethoven kept this under his piano: $\overline{2}\ \overline{7}\ \overline{26}\ \overline{12}\ \overline{1}\ \overline{4}\ \overline{17}\ \ \overline{15}\ \overline{14}\ \overline{19}$

2. In 1751, George Frideric Handel began losing his $\overline{18}\ \overline{8}\ \overline{6}\ \overline{7}\ \overline{19}$ and by 1753, he was totally $\overline{1}\ \overline{11}\ \overline{8}\ \overline{13}\ \overline{3}$.

3. Johannes Brahms became close friends with composers $\overline{2}\ \overline{11}\ \overline{26}\ \overline{17}\ \overline{26}$ and Robert Schumann.

4. Antonio Vivaldi was ordained as a priest in 1703, where his startling red hair earned him the nickname of " $\overline{19}\ \overline{7}\ \overline{4}\ \ \overline{17}\ \overline{4}\ \overline{3}\ \ \overline{15}\ \overline{17}\ \overline{8}\ \overline{4}\ \overline{18}\ \overline{19}$."

5. As a child, Bach learned the $\overline{21}\ \overline{8}\ \overline{14}\ \overline{11}\ \overline{8}\ \overline{13}$ from his father and the $\overline{2}\ \overline{11}\ \overline{26}\ \overline{21}\ \overline{8}\ \overline{2}\ \overline{7}\ \overline{14}\ \overline{17}\ \overline{3}$ from his brother.

6. By the time he was nine, Mozart had written several $\overline{18}\ \overline{14}\ \overline{13}\ \overline{26}\ \overline{19}\ \overline{26}\ \overline{18}$ and even his first $\overline{18}\ \overline{24}\ \overline{12}\ \overline{15}\ \overline{7}\ \overline{14}\ \overline{13}\ \overline{24}$.

7. Haydn had composed a mass by the age of $\overline{19}\ \overline{7}\ \overline{8}\ \overline{17}\ \overline{19}\ \overline{4}\ \overline{4}\ \overline{13}$.

8. This was one of Beethoven's favorite foods: $\overline{12}\ \overline{26}\ \overline{2}\ \overline{26}\ \overline{17}\ \overline{14}\ \overline{13}\ \overline{8}$ and $\overline{2}\ \overline{7}\ \overline{4}\ \overline{4}\ \overline{18}\ \overline{4}$.

© 2008 Heritage Music Press, a Lorenz company. All rights reserved.
This page may be reproduced for single-classroom use. This is a non-transferable license.

Name _____ Date _____ Teacher _____

Music Style Shuffle

August • Relaxation Day

Our music styles have been working so hard they've worked themselves into a jumble. Now that it's Relaxation Day, help them chill out by rearranging the letters in each group to spell a music style or era. The first one has been done for you.

1. WARABODY   =   b r o a (d) w a y
2. SLICCLASA =   _ (_) _ _ _ _ _ _
3. REQABOU   =   (_) _ _ _ _ _ _
4. SEBUL   =   _ _ _ _ (_)
5. PRA   =   _ (_) _
6. NAILT   =   _ _ (_) _ _
7. GNIWS   =   _ _ _ (_) _
8. TOMRACIN   =   _ _ _ _ _ (_) _ _
9. CORK   =   _ _ (_) _
10. KOLF   =   _ (_) _ _
11. HHOIPP   =   _ _ _ _ (_) _
12. YTUCRNO   =   _ _ _ (_) _ _ _
13. EGGARE   =   _ _ _ _ (_) _

Scratch Pad

Rearrange the circled letters from above to answer the question below.

What did Sue have for breakfast?   __ __ __ __ __

__ __ __ __ __ __ __

© 2008 Heritage Music Press, a Lorenz company. All rights reserved.
This page may be reproduced for single-classroom use. This is a non-transferable license.

Name _____ Date _____

Back to School

It is back-to-school time, and the band teacher is making sure all the instruments ar[e ready for the] new students. A list of all the instruments the students need is below. Help the teache[r get] ready by drawing a line from each of those instruments, which are piled at the bottom o[f the page,] to its shelf.

Teacher's List

- 1 tambourine
- 2 clarinets
- 1 trombone
- 1 triangle
- 1 pair of crash cymbals
- 1 flute

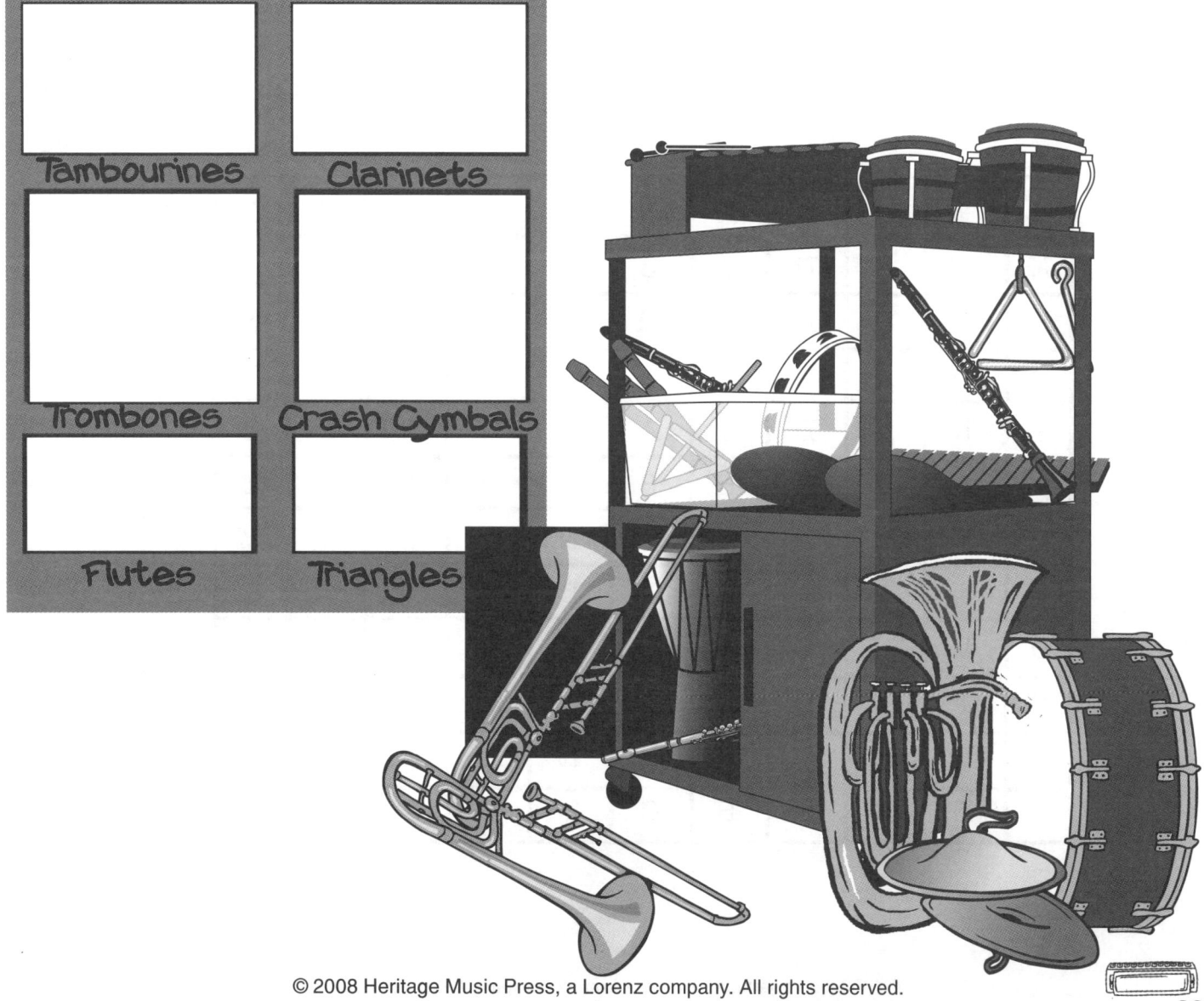

© 2008 Heritage Music Press, a Lorenz company. All rights reserved.
This page may be reproduced for single-classroom use. This is a non-transferable license.

Date_____ Teacher_____

Up, Down and All Around

August • Roller Coaster Day

Hidden in this grid are 22 well-known composers. The last names follow each other and twist and turn like a roller coaster through the grid. Once you discover the first name, you should be able to find the other 21. There are no extra letters and the words can be forwards or backwards. Try highlighting the words as you discover them and watch the track take shape.

Begin here and continue down each column.	Mendelssohn	Schubert	Debussy	Dvořák	Joplin
	Lehar	Vivaldi	Chopin	Grieg	Clementi
	Beethoven	Wagner	Brahms	Bartók	
	Mozart	Handel	Bach	Haydn	
	Purcell	Liszt	Borodin	Schumann	

L	E	H	A	R	B	E	E	T	H	O	V
N	W	A	U	S	B	O	R	T	L	I	E
H	I	G	B	S	H	R	A	O	P	N	N
O	D	N	E	Y	C	O	B	K	O	C	M
S	L	E	D	C	A	D	G	H	J	L	O
S	A	R	T	H	B	I	E	A	N	E	Z
L	V	H	Z	O	S	N	I	Y	N	M	A
E	I	A	S	P	M	D	R	D	A	E	R
D	V	N	I	I	H	V	G	N	M	N	T
N	T	D	L	N	A	O	K	S	U	T	P
E	R	E	L	B	R	R	A	C	H	I	U
M	E	B	U	H	C	S	L	L	E	C	R

40 © 2008 Heritage Music Press, a Lorenz company. All rights reserved. This page may be reproduced for single-classroom use. This is a non-transferable license.

Name _____ Date _____ Teacher _____

Know Your Notes Pumpkin Puzzler

September • First Day of Autumn

It's autumn and all the pumpkins are ready to be picked and carved. To carve your pumpkin face, get out your crayons, follow the directions below, and watch the face take shape.

Color the areas with treble clefs dark green.

Color the areas with dotted half notes light green.

Color the areas with half notes yellow.

Color the areas with quarter notes orange.

Color the areas with whole notes light orange.

© 2008 Heritage Music Press, a Lorenz company. All rights reserved.
This page may be reproduced for single-classroom use. This is a non-transferable license.

Name _____ Date _____ Teacher _____

It's Up...It's Good
September • Football Season

The leaves are beginning to change color, the air is getting cooler, and that can only mean one thing... Football Season! This season, our kicker is going to be busy making composer-fact field goals. Draw a line from each football through the goal post of the composer being described in the fact. You may want to use a different color for each composer. When you are finished, total each composer's field goals and see who scored the most points.

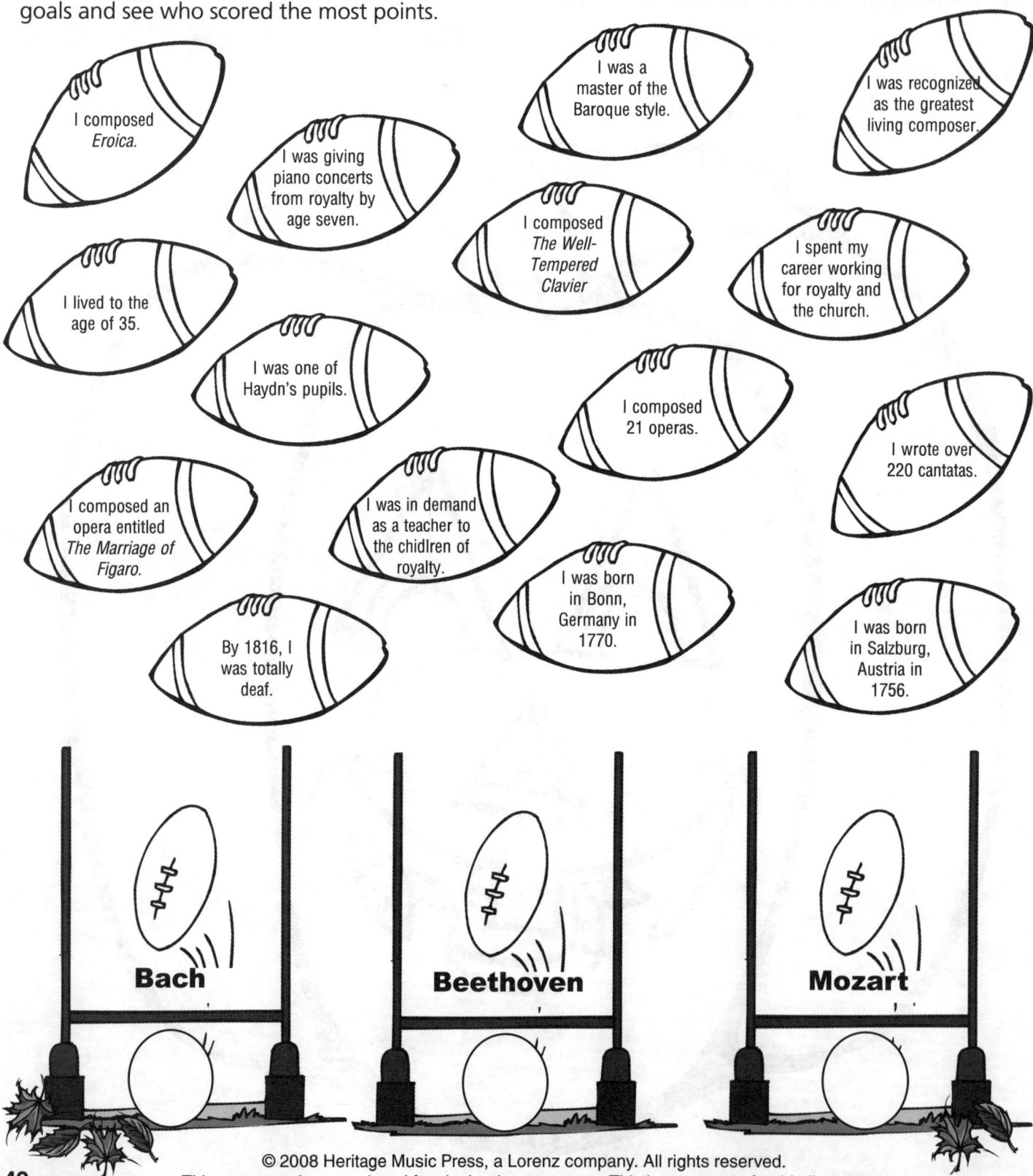

42

© 2008 Heritage Music Press, a Lorenz company. All rights reserved.
This page may be reproduced for single-classroom use. This is a non-transferable license.

Name _____ Date _____ Teacher _____

No Work, Just Play for Labor Day

September

Name each of the notes below to learn some interesting things about Labor Day.

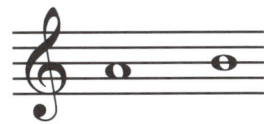

1. L ____ ____ O R Day is observed on the first Monday in September.

2. The first Labor Day C ____ L ____ ____ R A T I O N took place in the city of New York in 1882.

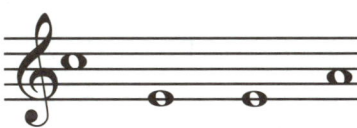

3. In 1887, Oregon ____ ____ ____ ____ M E the first state to make Labor Day a legal holiday.

4. In 1894, President Grover ____ L ____ V ____ L ____ N D signed a bill making Labor Day a national holiday.

5. Labor Day has come to symbolize the end of summer and the beginning of ____ ____ L L.

6. Labor Day honors all working people. It was Peter J. McGuire who first

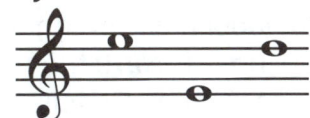

suggested a N ____ ____ ____ for the holiday.

© 2008 Heritage Music Press, a Lorenz company. All rights reserved.
This page may be reproduced for single-classroom use. This is a non-transferable license.

Date_____ Teacher_____

Hispanic Music and Musicians

National Hispanic Heritage Month

Find the words listed at the bottom of the page in the puzzle below. They are hidden horizontally, vertically and diagonally, both forward and backward. For the terms that are made up of multiple words—all of the words are included in the puzzle, run together without spaces.

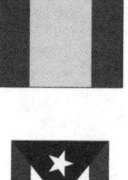

```
B P U L N B Z M F D N J M A R I A C H I Y U C
H Q A K H G X N L G R Y Z Y X W T S R Q U V H
Y S D L Y T G U A N T A N A M E R A M N B V R
E X F J M R C B M K T V V A P P A X S J K L I
L C G H U A V V E L E W H L J L M K A B M A S
J A H M J F S C N J Q C P K F A Q W R A A B T
A R O B M A T X C G A A I J O C N J E D N C I
R L J E I V B Z O R S R U H I I W E H E U F N
A O K D K C N X A D F B Y G J D B H C H E G A
B S L C O D E C O L O R E S N O E R N I L J A
E S Q R L D U V F V H N T A H D V G A L D K G
T A W F P C M B D I K K R X B O R T R M E N U
A N E V A E S N S H N U E S G M C F V P F O I
P T R L T W P K A U V R W C V I T Y T Q A R L
A A T T I S A J X E L Q D F N X D C T L S E
T N Y G T X N H T L Z P L F C G Z U U U L V R
I A N T O N I O C A R L O S J O B I M X A W A
O D U B P Z S Y G A C Z K V D T Y S B Y Z V E
U E I Y U A H U N A S X J G X R U I I T Q G D
J R O H E Q G I K W B T H B S E A Z A R A Y C
M E R I N G U E Y R M T A H Z W I S B F S H X
N T P N T W I Q E Y L R M N A Q L W C C W N S
M Y X U E E T M A I K H N W E A S K D X E U W
K U C J I R A N C P R N B T S T O M E D D J Q
O I V M K T R H U M B A G H J K S L P O I U Y
```

___ Christina Aguilera
___ Castanets
___ Cumbia
___ Placido Domingo
___ De Colores
___ El Jarabe Tapatío
___ Manuel de Falla
___ Flamenco
___ Guantanamera
___ Antonio Carlos Jobim
___ La Cucaracha
___ Mariachi

___ Meringue
___ Palmas
___ Tito Puente
___ Rancheras
___ Rhumba
___ Salsa
___ Samba
___ Carlos Santana
___ Spanish guitar
___ Tambor
___ Vihuela

Bonus Activity

In the blank to the left of each word, label it according to the following list. *Hint:* the number after each category tells you how many of each is in the list.

1. Performer and/or composer (6)
2. Type of music and/or dance (9)
3. Traditional folk song (4)
4. Instrument (4)

© 2008 Heritage Music Press, a Lorenz company. All rights reserved.
This page may be reproduced for single-classroom use. This is a non-transferable license.

Name _____ Date _____ Teacher _____

Spot the Difference

October • Make a Difference Day

To celebrate Make a Difference Day, find and circle the things that are different in each set of pictures below. When you are finished, turn your paper over and make a list of things you could do to make a difference in someone's life.

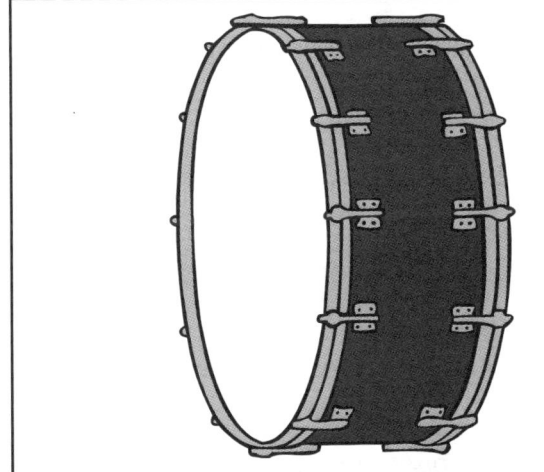 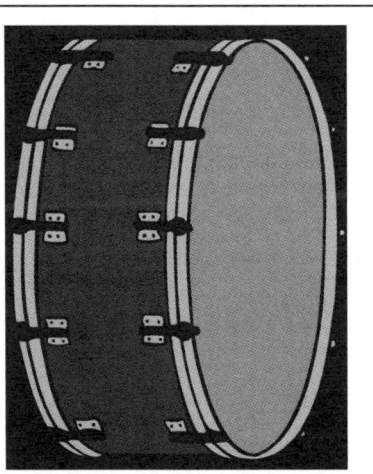

© 2008 Heritage Music Press, a Lorenz company. All rights reserved.
This page may be reproduced for single-classroom use. This is a non-transferable license.

Name _____ Date _____ Teacher _____

Trick or Treat?

October • Halloween

It's Halloween! Let's see how many treats you can get. Below are some facts about various music topics. Some are true and some are a trick. See if you can find all the facts that are a trick. Fill in the appropriate circle beside each fact.

Trick (false) **Treat** (true)

○ ○ 1. All of the instruments in the string family are chordophones.

○ ○ 2. A harp has 57 strings.

○ ○ 3. All woodwind instruments use air to create sound.

○ ○ 4. The piccolo is a cousin of the saxophone.

○ ○ 5. Woodwind instruments are classified as Idiophones.

○ ○ 6. The tuba is the biggest and highest sounding instrument in the brass family.

○ ○ 7. A trumpet uses a slide to change pitches.

○ ○ 8. Percussion instruments can be pitched or nonpitched.

○ ○ 9. A xylophone is part of the keyboard family.

○ ○ 10. All brass instruments are played with the right hand.

○ ○ 11. The sound quality of brass instruments can be changed by using a mute, which is placed in or over the instrument's mouthpiece.

○ ○ 12. The percussion family is the largest of all the instrument families.

○ ○ 13. A cello is smaller than a string bass, but bigger than a viola.

○ ○ 14. Conga drums are a pitched instrument.

15. A glockenspiel is a metal, pitched percussion instrument.

© 2008 Heritage Music Press, a Lorenz company. All rights reserved.
This page may be reproduced for single-classroom use. This is a non-transferable license.

Name _____ Date _____ Teacher _____

Style Search

October • Sweetest Day

Is there a style of music that you think is sweet? See if you can find these sweet styles of music listed below. Circle each one as you find it in the puzzle. The words can be straight across, up and down, diagonal, or even backwards. When you are finished, write down your favorite style and why you think it is sweet!

```
I E F S M R M R A U U E O O R
Y R O C K A N D R O L L T A Z
C T E T Z P X K O O A S G P D
J A B O J O Z P H X C T V V R
W E Q C S L W H M N I V C H T
N H G E O P R J C M S Z Z H W
I T U I P U K Q E Y S J G X C
C L T Z M G N L W H A T G O T
B A U Z C F H T O N L R M A K
Q C L A S S I C R O C K F K V
S I W J S D P E U Y R Q B G T
Z S L F W O H X D X W C F W Q
H U P G P E O Q T K F L X M S
Z M H O A R P T X X K P M D G
Q Q B K N G S E H X X L I L Q
```

Blues
Classical
Classic Rock
Country
HipHop
Jazz
Musical Theatre
Pop
Ragtime
Rap
Rock and Roll

My favorite style of music is...

_____
_____
_____
_____
_____
_____

© 2008 Heritage Music Press, a Lorenz company. All rights reserved.
This page may be reproduced for single-classroom use. This is a non-transferable license.

Name _____ Date _____ Teacher _____

Define to Find

October • Dictionary Day

Facts about several important composers are listed below, but there's a word missing in each. Your task on this Dictionary Day is to supply the missing word. Don't worry, a "Definition Bank" is included if you need help. Read each definition listed there and think of the word it defines to build your own word bank.

1. William Grant Still studied _____ at Wilberforce University.

2. William Grant Still dropped out of Wilberforce University. Later he continued his education at Oberlin and studied _____.

3. By the age of two, Amy Beach was _____ melodies to complement songs her mother sang to her.

4. Josquin Des Pres was a master of _____.

5. Haydn's music career began at age 8, when he became a _____ boy.

6. Bach spent his career working for royalty and the church, which meant writing "on _____." In other words, his bosses would tell him what to write.

7. Bach came from a musical family. His brother and father were _____ musicians.

8. Wolfgang Amadeus Mozart's piano concertos were _____.

9. Beethoven was very good at both playing and music _____. Because of this, he was also given composition lessons.

10. Brahm's was influenced by the great German composers that came before him. Because of this, his music is warm and expressive, a quality of the Romantic Period, but also very _____, a quality of the Classical Period.

DEFINITION BANK

- When someone has a lot of experience and great skill. If you do something as your job and get paid for it. _____
- This means "many sounds." Partner songs are a simple example of this texture. _____
- A set of statements or principles that help explain how things work. _____
- This helps sick people get well. Ususally, a doctor tells you what kind to take. _____
- A word meaning organized or put together very systematically. _____
- The art of arranging sound. _____
- When a musician is composing on the spur of the moment. _____
- When your teacher gives you work to do, it is called this. _____
- This means to change the way people view or treat something. _____
- The name for a group of singers. _____

© 2008 Heritage Music Press, a Lorenz company. All rights reserved.
This page may be reproduced for single-classroom use. This is a non-transferable license.

Name _____ Date _____ Teacher _____

A Very Verdi Day

October • Verdi's Birthday

One of the greatest opera composers of all time is Giuseppe Verdi (Juh-SEP-pee VEAR-dee). Verdi was born in 1813 in Italy. Today, we celebrate his birthday on both the 9th and the 10th of October because no one is sure which of those dates is his actual birthday. (Wouldn't it be cool to have two birthdays?)

Operas have been written about everything from love to important events in history to imaginary lands far away. Imagine the story you would tell in an opera. What is it about? Who are some of the characters? Can you think of a title? Now imagine your opera is being performed at the famous *La Scala* opera house in Milan, Italy. Create the poster that will hang outside the theater and announce your opera to the world.

Logo is a trademark of Teatro alla Scala, Milan, Italy. Its appearance here does not constitute an endorsement.

© 2008 Heritage Music Press, a Lorenz company. All rights reserved.
This page may be reproduced for single-classroom use. This is a non-transferable license.

Name _____ Date _____ Teacher _____

Take a Hike

November • Take a Hike Day

There are plenty of places to "hold" and see the sights on this hike. If you find and follow the music symbol that means to hold, it will help you find your way. When you reach the end go back and count how many of these symbols you passed and write that number in the space provided.

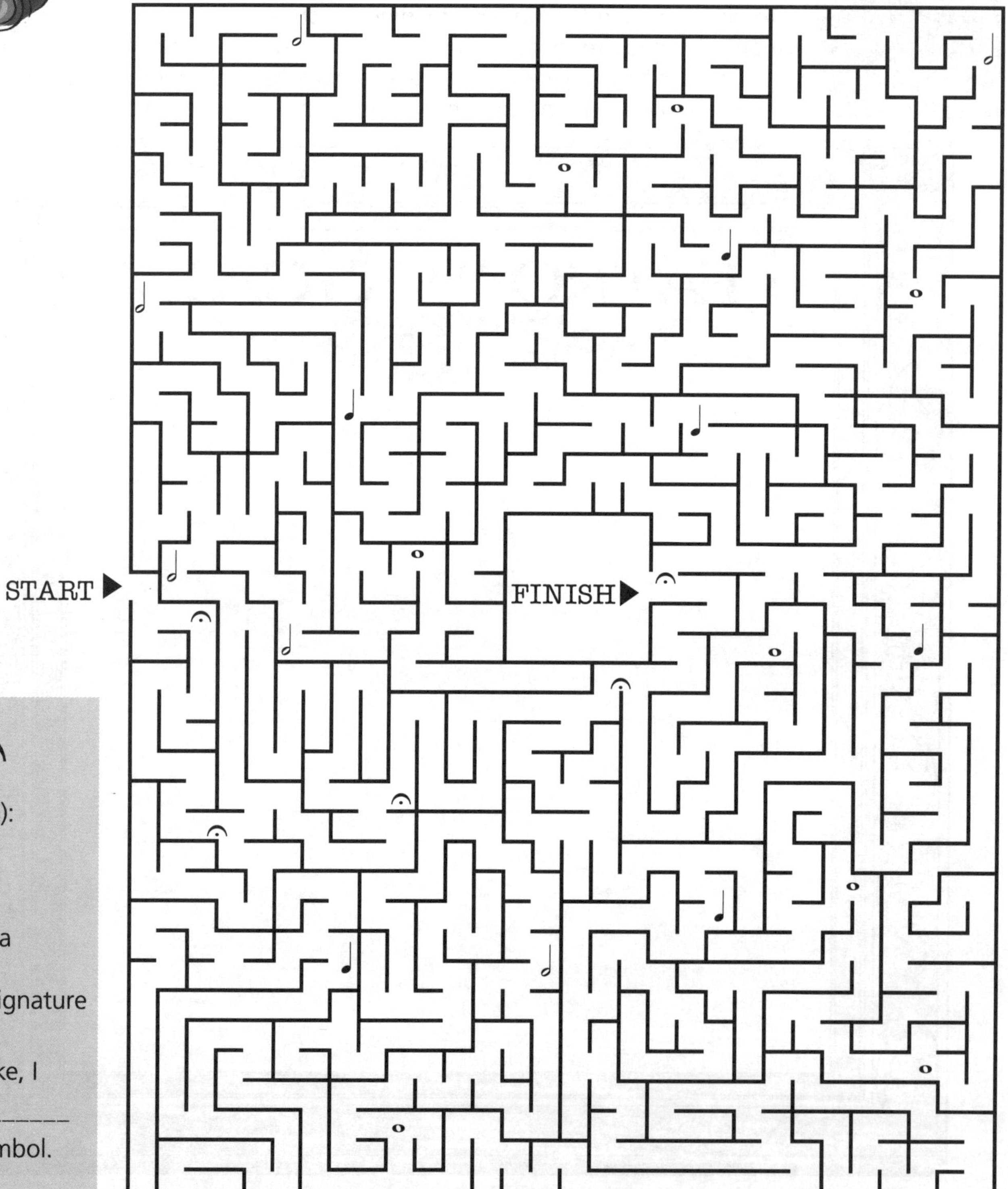

This is a(n):

A. Accent

B. Fermata

C. Time Signature

On my hike, I passed _____ of this symbol.

© 2008 Heritage Music Press, a Lorenz company. All rights reserved.
This page may be reproduced for single-classroom use. This is a non-transferable license.

Name _____ Date _____ Teacher _____

Let's Talk Turkey

November • Thanksgiving

Our Thanksgiving turkeys have lost their tail feathers. Each turkey is marked with one of the four instrument families. See if you can help the turkeys get their feathers back by drawing a line from the instrument to its family.

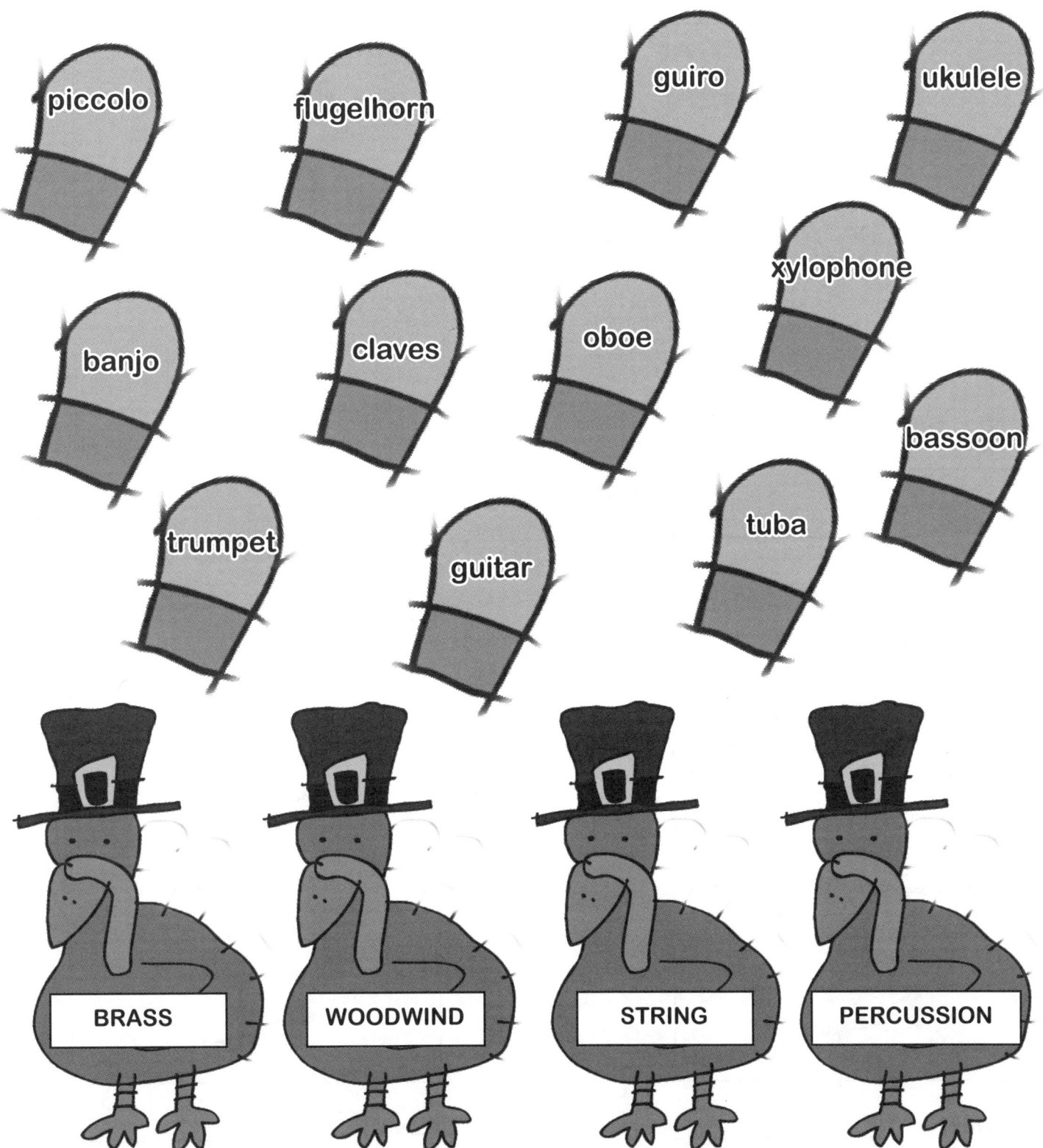

© 2008 Heritage Music Press, a Lorenz company. All rights reserved.
This page may be reproduced for single-classroom use. This is a non-transferable license.

Name _____ Date _____ Teacher _____

Brain Busters

November • Use Less Stuff Day

For Use Less Stuff Day, we decided to use less words. *Brain Busters* are puzzles using pictures to illustrate music concepts. As you try to solve each, be sure to think creatively, and check out the puzzle category in the bottom right corner of each puzzle. Knowing that will be a big help!

Puzzle #1

Answer: _____

Puzzle #2

Answer: _____

Puzzle #3

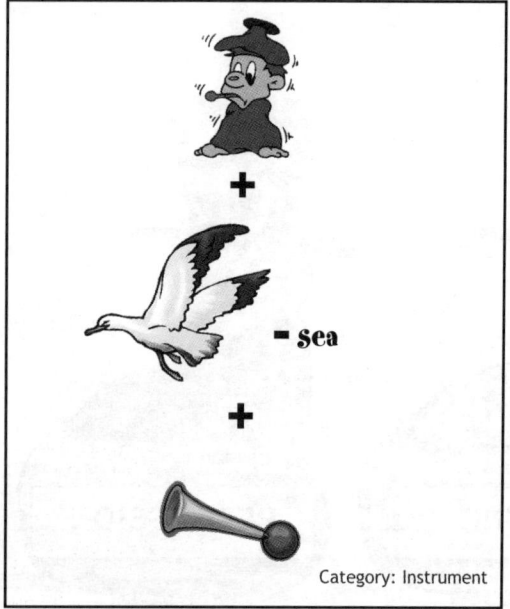

Answer: _____

Puzzle #4

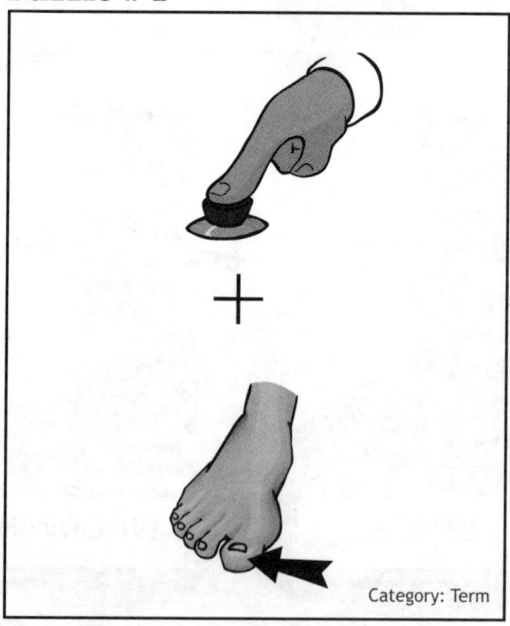

Answer: _____

© 2008 Heritage Music Press, a Lorenz company. All rights reserved.
This page may be reproduced for single-classroom use. This is a non-transferable license.

Name _____ Date _____ Teacher _____

Sandwich Stacker

November • National Sandwich Day

It's National Sandwich Day. Let's celebrate by using our note-reading skills to build some tasty sandwiches!

Each of our sandwich ingredients has its own note:

Note name:	A	B	C	D	E	F	G
Ingredient:	Turkey	Ham	Roast Beef	Swiss Cheese	American Cheese	Tomato	Lettuce

Start by reading the notes in each sandwich on the left and writing what's on it in the blanks to the right.

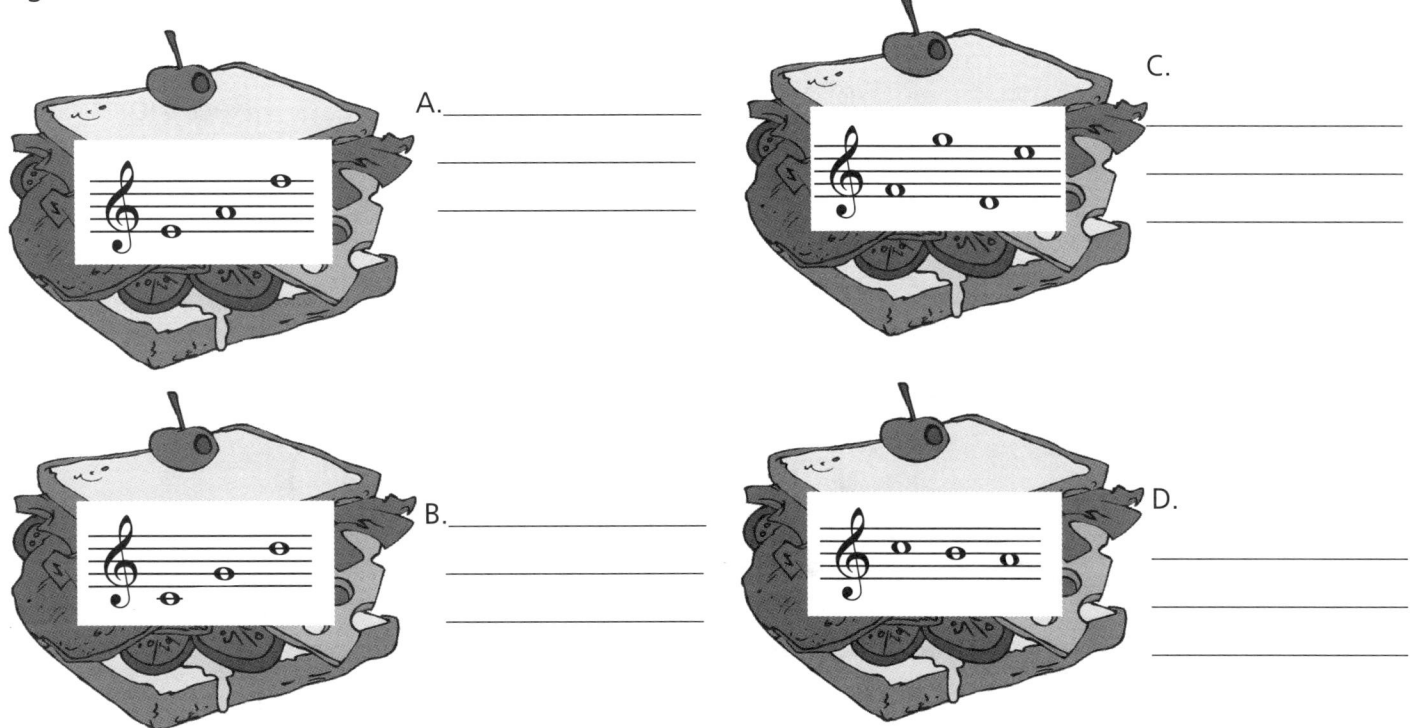

Now, it's your turn to build a few sandwiches. Read the ingredients and write the corresponding note of each on the staff provided.

Ingredients

Ham and Swiss

Turkey, Tomato and Lettuce

Roast Beef, Ham and Lettuce

Ham, American Cheese and Tomato

Here's your sandwich!

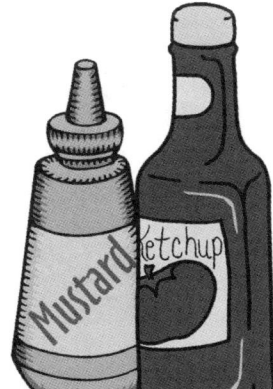

My favorite type of sandwich is: _____

© 2008 Heritage Music Press, a Lorenz company. All rights reserved.
This page may be reproduced for single-classroom use. This is a non-transferable license.

Name _____ Date _____ Teacher _____

Trim the Tree

December • Christmas

The holidays are coming and we need to decorate our Christmas tree! Color all the ornaments according to the directions on the right. If you have time, color the tree, too.

Color all the...
Eighth notes = Red
Quarter notes = Blue
Half notes = Orange
Dotted half notes = Gray
Whole notes = Purple
Eighth rests = Pink
Quarter rests = Light Blue
Half rests = Yellow
Whole rests = Red Violet

54 © 2008 Heritage Music Press, a Lorenz company. All rights reserved.
This page may be reproduced for single-classroom use. This is a non-transferable license.

Name _____ Date _____ Teacher _____

Cookie Count

December • National Cookie Day

Great news! It's National Cookie Day and our teacher is bringing in cookies to celebrate. But before we can eat we have to help make sure that each tray of cookies includes a dozen beats if counted in 4/4 time. Some trays may have too many beats, some too few. If there are too many beats, cross out the notes or rests until only 12 remain. If there aren't enough beats, add notes or rests until there are 12.

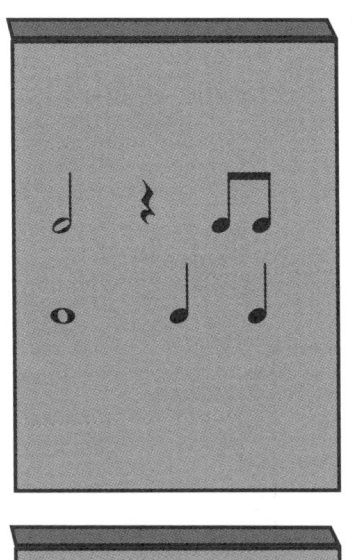
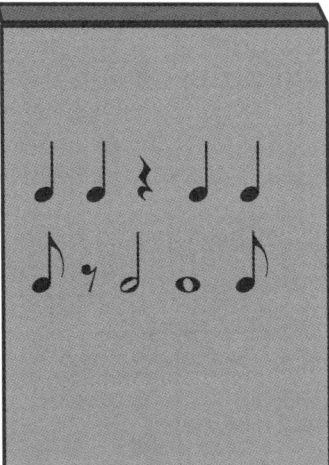

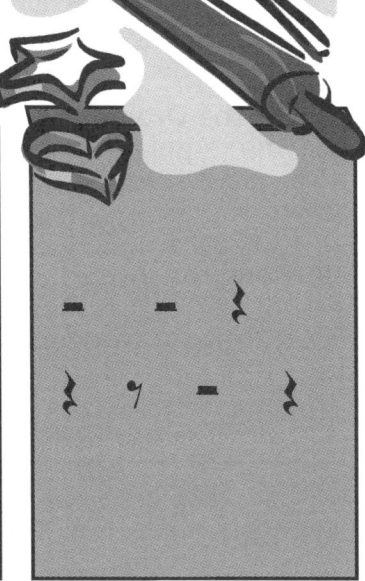
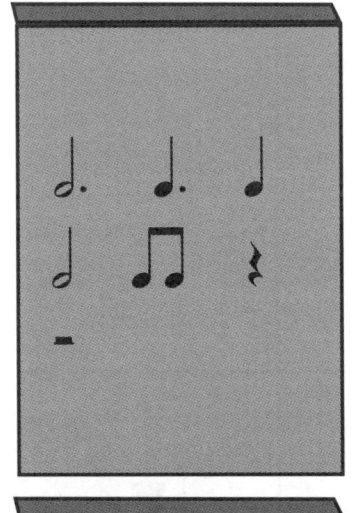
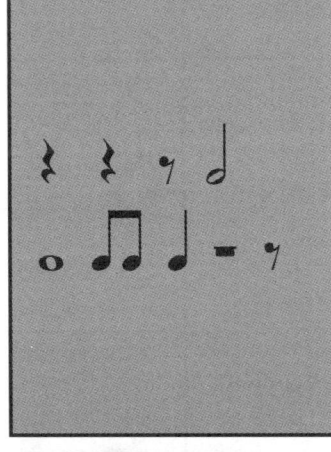
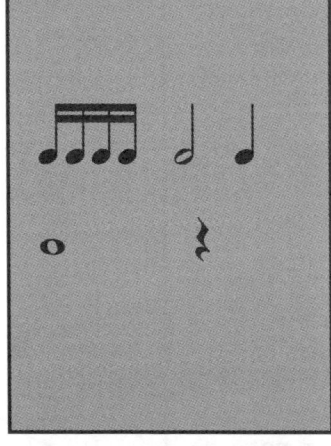
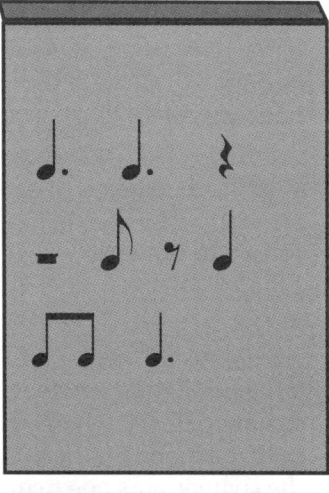
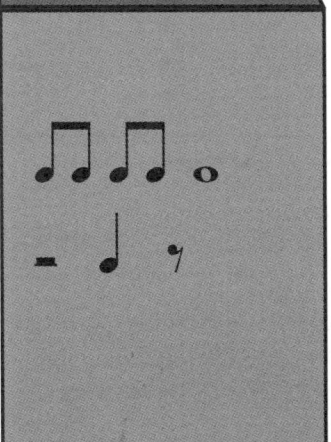
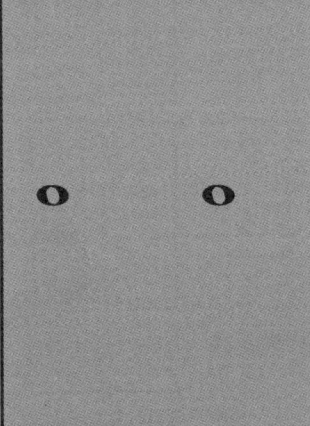
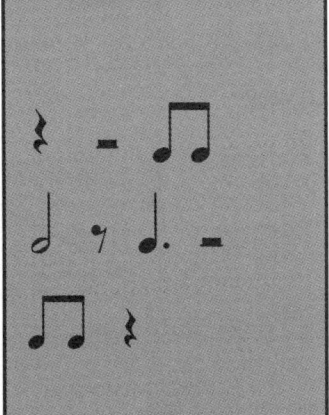

Name _____ Date _____ Teacher _____

Music Note Dreidel

December • Hanukkah

The traditional Hanukkah game of dreidel is played in homes all over the world. The Hebrew word for dreidel is sevivon, which means "to turn around." Dreidels have a Hebrew letter on each of their four sides. Together they stand for the phrase "Nes gadol hayah sham," which means "a great miracle occurred there." Use the template below to create your own dreidel using music notes.

Making the Dreidel:
Copy the template found on this page for each of the students. You may want to enlarge to 125%. Have students decorate the dreidel, then cut it out. Cut an X in the tiny rectangle where shown.

Fold along the inside lines, making a top shape. Glue the flaps inside the top.

Stick a straw or wooden dowel through the X you cut at the top and push it gently to the bottom of the dreidel.

How to Play Music Note Dreidel

1. Any number of players can take part in the game. Each player begins the game with an equal number of markers (around 20). Objects such as pennies, nuts, chocolate chips or raisins work well.

2. At the beginning of each round, each player puts two game pieces into the center, or pot.

3. The first player spins the dreidel. If it lands on the rest, nothing happens. If it lands on the whole note, the spinner gets the whole pot; on the half note, half; and on the quarter note, the spinner puts one item in the pot. Continue in this way, with each player getting the chance to spin.

4. When the pot is empty, each player puts two items in and the game continues. If a player is out of markers, they are "out" or they may ask a fellow player for a loan. The winner is the player who collects all of the markers.

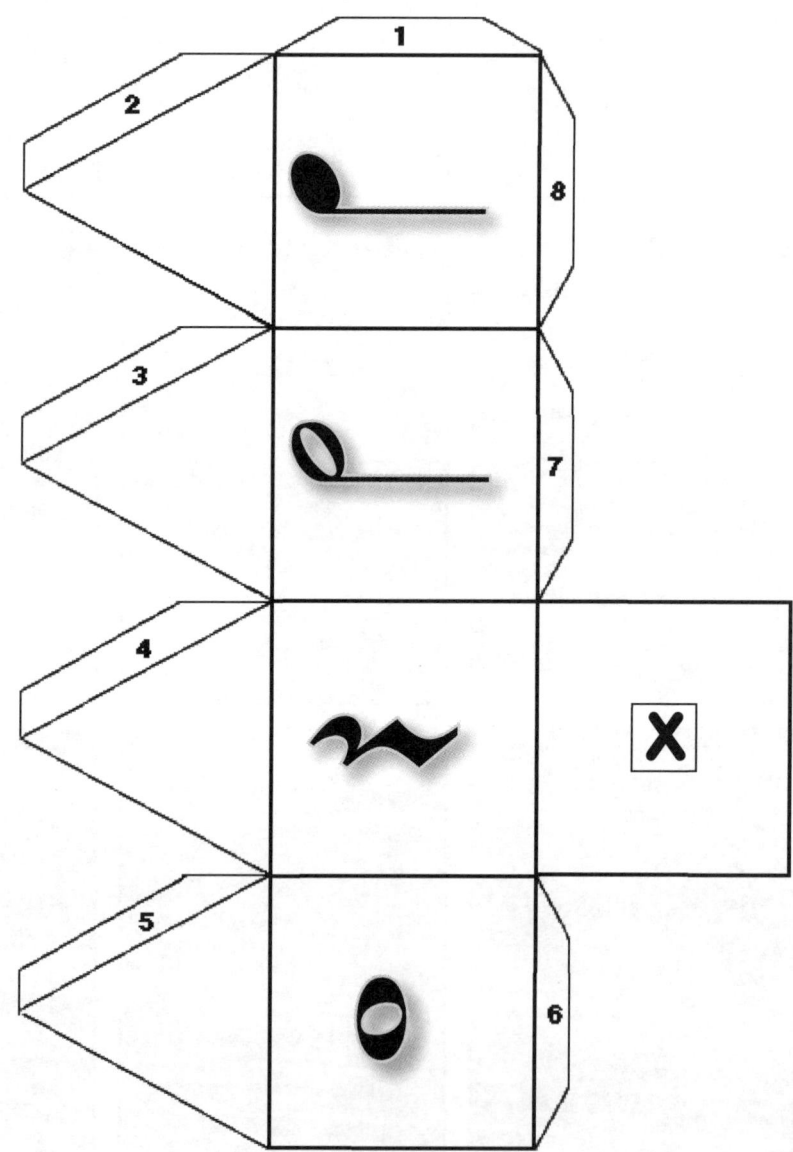

© 2008 Heritage Music Press, a Lorenz company. All rights reserved.
This page may be reproduced for single-classroom use. This is a non-transferable license.

Name _____ Date _____ Teacher _____

What's the word?

December • First Crossword Puzzle

Did you know that on December 21, 1913 the first crossword puzzle was published in the newspaper? To celebrate this fun day, we created our own crossword puzzle. See how many music terms you know by answering the questions below to solve the puzzle.

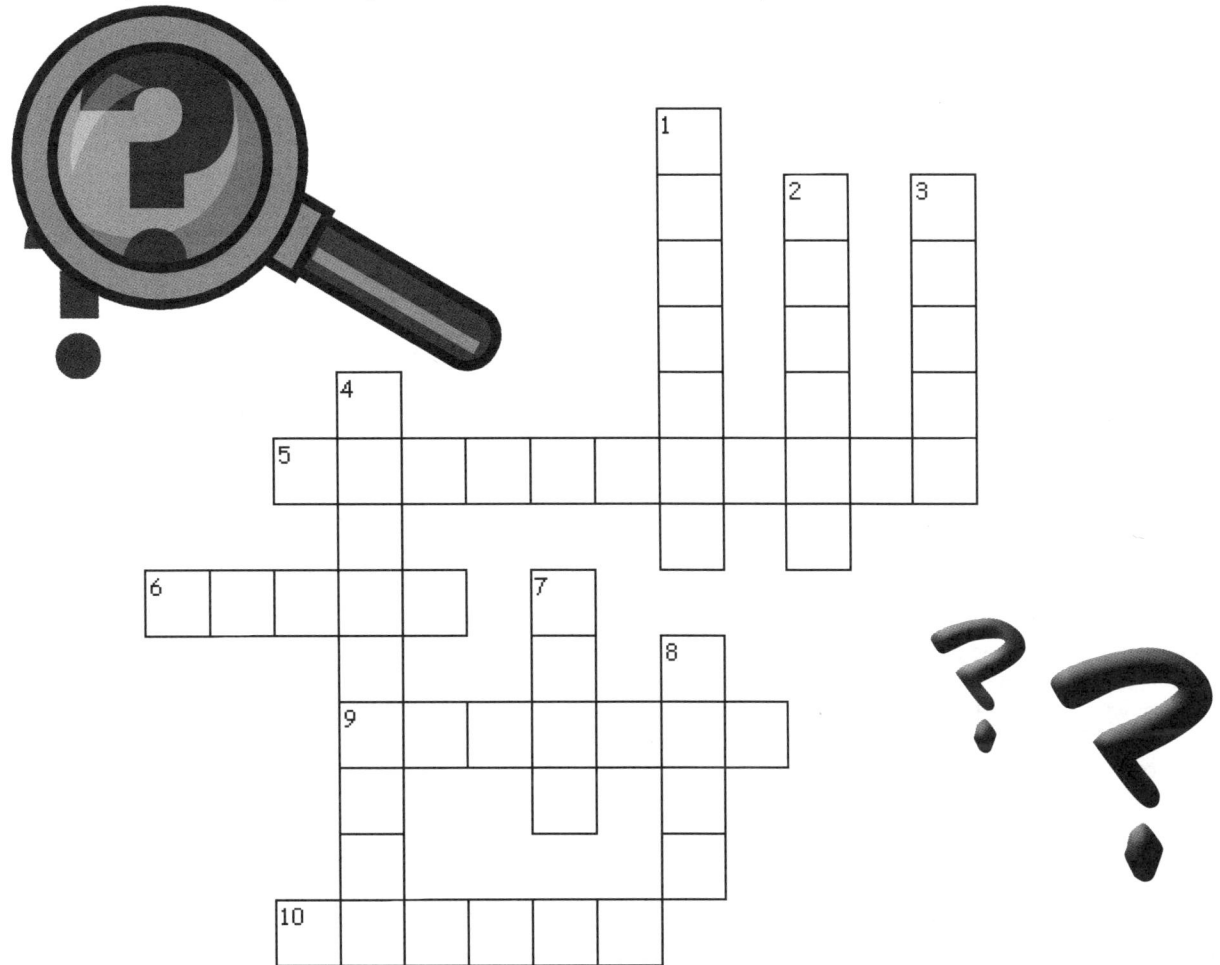

Across
5. Gradually becoming softer.
6. Three or more tones sounded simultaneously.
9. The symbol that indicates a note is neither sharp nor flat.
10. To play or sing groups of notes smoothly.

Down
1. To direct a group of musicians.
2. To emphasize a note.
3. The speed of a section of a composition.
4. An adjustable device that indicates the exact tempo of a piece.
7. A curved line notated above two or more notes that indicates they are to be played *legato*.
8. Italian for head, and the "C" in *D.C. al Fine*, it refers to the beginning of a piece.

Fact Sheets

Composers

JOSQUIN DES PRES (C. 1450–1521)

One of the most important composers of the Renaissance (REN-uh-sahnss), Josquin des Pres (JAHS-scan deh PRAY) was a member of the Flemish School, which is the name of a group of composers who lived and worked in Flanders. (Can't find Flanders on your globe? That's because it became part of what are now Belgium and Northern France.) No one is sure of Josquin's exact birth date, but most scholars think he was born around 1450. We also don't know a lot about his life. He lived in Flanders but as more and more people heard his music, he was invited to work in Milan, Italy, and in Rome for the Pope. He also lived in several places in France. Although there is a lot we don't know, what we do know is that until his death in 1521, Josquin wrote a lot of really great music! Josquin was a master of *polyphony*, which means "many sounds." Have you ever sung a partner song? This is a song where some people sing one melody at the same time others are singing a different melody. Partner songs are a very simple example of polyphony. When Josquin first began composing, if you liked a piece that he wrote, you had to get his original and recopy it yourself, by hand. But then, in 1500, something big happened—a man named Petrucci printed the first piece of music. Petrucci continued printing music, a lot of which was by Josquin. In fact, Josquin was the first composer in history to have a printed book that included all of his pieces, and only his pieces.

JOHANN SEBASTIAN BACH (1685–1750)

J.S. Bach, who was born on March 21, 1685, in Eisenach, Germany, is the most important composer of the Baroque (bah-ROHK) Period. (It's no coincidence that Bach died in 1750 and the Baroque period ends in 1750.) So how did Bach get so good? For one, Bach's father and older brother (not to mention his grandfather and great-grandfather) were professional musicians. Not only did they teach Bach to play the violin and organ, the family connections meant that Bach was constantly around music and important musicians. It also meant that Bach's family supported him when he said he wanted to become a professional musician himself. A lot of other composers didn't have such supportive families; they often had to study other subjects or enter other professions and compose on the side. In addition to his family and his talent, Bach also "got good" by practicing a lot. He would find music written by composers that he admired and copy it note for note. This helped him learn the rules of composing. It also introduced him to music from other places, like Italy and France, which became important influences on his personal style. Like most composers in the Baroque Period, Bach spent his career working for royalty and the church, which meant writing "on assignment." Just like your teacher gives you assignments, Bach's bosses would tell him, "I need a piece for this event," and he would have to write it. And he wrote a lot—over 220 cantatas, which are works for choir and orchestra; numerous keyboard collections, including *The Well-Tempered Clavier*; chamber music, including his *Musical Offering*; and orchestral works, including the *Brandenburg Concertos*.

GEORGE FRIDERIC HANDEL (1685–1759)

The second-most-famous Baroque composer (Handel's bad luck for composing in the same period as one of the greatest masters of all time, J.S. Bach), George Frideric Handel (George FREE-der-ich HAHN-dul) was one of the first composers who was able to make a living solely as a composer. Born in Germany in 1685, Handel was trained as an organist and worked as a choir master there before moving to London, England, when he was 25. Handel loved England and stayed there for the rest of his life. (He's even buried at Westminster Abbey, an honor reserved for only the most famous Brits.) Although he wrote a lot of instrumental music and vocal solos, Handel's first musical love was opera. He wrote more than 40 of them, but unfortunately the kind of operas that he liked to write—more serious operas in an Italian style called *opera seria*—were becoming less and less popular with the English people. Problem was, Handel was living a very extravagant life and composing was his only job. He needed a hit, and quick. Handel found his "hit" in the form of oratorios. Oratorios are extended choral works about a religious subject that have an orchestral accompaniment. They are like operas in that they tell a story with song and there are characters, but unlike opera, the performers don't wear costumes and they don't act out the story. The most famous of Handel's oratorios is *Messiah*, which includes one of the most famous pieces of classical music—"Hallelujah Chorus."

Fact Sheets

Composers

WOLFGANG AMADEUS MOZART (1756–1791)

Born in Salzburg, Austria, Mozart is one of the greatest composers in all of Classical and classical music. A true prodigy, he was giving piano concerts for the royalty of Europe by age seven. By age nine, he had written his first *symphony*. (A symphony is a piece for orchestra that includes several sections, called movements.) By the time he was a teenager, Mozart was living the pop star life. He was constantly on tour, performing and conducting in front of huge audiences the pieces he'd written. In his short life—he lived only 35 years—Mozart composed every *form*, or type, of music that was important in the Classical Period. These include the symphony, mass, opera, string quartet, and sonata and concerto, both of which are multi-movement works for a solo instrument. Mozart's piano concertos were revolutionary, meaning they changed the way other composers treated the form. Many of his 41 symphonies are still performed today, as are several of his 21 operas, including *The Marriage of Figaro* and *Cosi fan tutti*. These works showcase his gift for writing wonderful melodies, or tunes. One of his most famous melodies is *Eine kleine Nachtmusik*, or "A Little Night Music."

FRANZ JOSEPH HAYDN (1732–1809)

Haydn's music career began at age 8, when he became a choir boy at St. Stephen's in Vienna, Austria. After his voice changed and he had to leave the choir, Haydn worked as a music teacher and accompanist. Unfortunately, these jobs didn't pay very well and Haydn was very, very poor. All that changed when Prince Paul Esterházy hired Haydn to be a staff musician at his palace. For the next 30 years, Haydn no longer had to worry about where his next meal would come from, but he did have his hands full—he conducted the orchestra, directed the operas, played for dinner parties and other events, was in charge of all the musicians who worked at the palace, and had to write new pieces almost constantly. Because the Esterházy's palace was the place to be, Haydn's music was heard by lots and lots of people. As a result (and because his music was good), Haydn became one of the most famous musicians around. He was even friends with Mozart and was a teacher of Beethoven's. In fact, Haydn is often called "Papa" Haydn because he was such a big influence on Mozart and Beethoven, particularly when it came to their symphonies and string quartets. Unfortunately though, because he is thought of primarily as an influence on greater composers, the excellence of Haydn's many compositions, which include more than 100 symphonies, 80 string quartets, 20 operas, 14 masses, and numerous oratorios, including *The Creation*, is often overlooked.

LUDWIG VAN BEETHOVEN (1770–1827)

Ludwig van Beethoven was born on December 17, 1770 in Bonn, Germany. Born into a musical family—his grandfather was a choir master and his father was an amateur musician—Beethoven studied the violin, piano and horn. When he was young, all piano students learned theory, or the rules for how music is organized. Because Beethoven was very good at both playing and theory he was also given composition lessons. He was good at that, too. So good that his first published piece was written when he was just 12 years old! In 1790, Beethoven moved to Vienna. This city in Austria was home to a lot of composers, including Mozart and Franz Joseph Hadyn, with whom Beethoven took lessons. Haydn composed in a Classical style, and early on, Beethoven did too, writing lighter melodies with simple harmonies and textures, but he sometimes broke the established rules. As he developed as a composer, Beethoven started to break more and more rules. By 1804, Beethoven had completed his Symphony No. 3. Called the *Eroica*, or *Heroic*, this symphony changed the history of music. Symphony No. 3 was the longest symphony written to date—two or three times longer than any of Mozart's or Haydn's. The rhythms were more complex than his earlier works, and the music itself was also more expressive and emotional—two important characteristics of the period that followed the Classical. Called the Romantic, Beethoven's music laid the foundation for this style. Around the time he was writing Symphony No. 3, Beethoven started to lose his hearing. It got gradually worse and by 1816, he was totally deaf. Amazingly, he continued to compose, writing two more symphonies and several string quartet and piano concertos. Long before that, though, Beethoven was recognized as the greatest living composer. He was in demand as a concert performer and as a teacher to the children of royalty. This celebrity and reputation continued until his death in March of 1827.

Fact Sheets

Composers

JOHANNES BRAHMS (1833–1897)

Continuing the trend of musicians who went into the family business, Brahms's father was professional double bass player. He recognized his son's gift for music so began teaching him piano and eventually sent him for formal training. By the time he was 13, Brahms was playing piano professionally in theaters and taverns. Thanks in part to his family connections, Brahms was introduced to the composer Robert Schumann and his wife, Clara. Schumann was immediately impressed with Brahms, which was great because in addition to writing music, Schumann was a well-respected music journalist. When he wrote an article calling someone "a genius," which he did in Brahms's case, it was a big deal. Even with this kind of support, Brahms wasn't immediately successful as a composer. His first big piece, a piano sonata, was considered a failure, and it took ten years until he really had a "hit." That hit was his *German Requiem*, and it remains very popular today. Other hits include his string quartets; piano pieces, including his *Hungarian Dances*; sonatas for various solo instruments, including horn, clarinet and piano; songs and song cycles (which are sets of songs designed to be performed together); and his four symphonies. His symphonies were actually such big hits that when people heard them they thought, "finally, the next Beethoven!" Brahms is definitely a Romantic Period composer, but his style is much different than a lot of other Romantic composers. Brahms was very much influenced by the great German composers who came before him, particularly Bach and Beethoven. So while Brahms's music is warm and expressive (qualities of the Romantic Period) it is also very structured (which are qualities more associated with the Classical Period). In some ways, Brahms's music is similar to his personality. The man who preferred flannel shirts to formal dress, enjoyed beer, kept his house tidy, and whose manuscripts were always neat and easy-to-read, created well-structured, technically precise music that isn't flashy but is always memorable, even comfortable.

AMY BEACH (1867–1944)

Like another famous composer, Amy Beach was a prodigy. She could sing 40 songs—on pitch—by the time she was one. By two she was improvising melodies to complement songs her mother sang to her, and by four she was writing songs in her head and playing them on the piano. (Do you know the most famous music prodigy? It's Mozart!) Beach made her professional debut when she was 16 as a pianist with the Boston Symphony Orchestra. Her concert career was limited, as her husband asked that she not travel a lot, but this meant that she had more time to compose. (After her husband's death in 1910, Beach returned to the concert stage, touring the U.S. and Europe.) An American (she was born in New Hampshire and spent her life in the Northeast), much of Beach's music is nationalistic, or strongly influenced by the country where it's from. One example is her Symphony in E, "Gaelic," which is inspired by Boston, many of whose residents were Irish immigrants. In addition to a few other extended orchestral and choral works, Beach wrote chamber music, music for piano, and more than 120 songs. She also wrote articles about composition and the teaching of music.

WILLIAM GRANT STILL (1895–1978)

William Grant Still began his college education at Wilberforce University in Ohio as a student of medicine. He dropped out of school at Wilberforce, married, then continued his education at Oberlin, this time as a music student. His Oberlin education was interrupted in 1918 to serve in the U.S. Navy, after which he returned to his studies, this time at the New England Conservatory. A well-rounded musician, Still, who studied the violin as a young man, joined the String Quartet at Wilberforce and eventually taught himself to play all of the instruments of the string family, as well as the oboe, clarinet and saxophone. Often referred to as Dean of Negro Composers, the great conductor Leopold Stokowski adds to the case that Still is better labeled Dean of American Composers, saying "[he is] one of our greatest American composers. He has made a real contribution to music." Still's 150 compositions include nine operas, solo piano and chamber works, spiritual arrangements, and five symphonies, including his best-known work, *Afro-American Symphony*. Like many 20th-century composers, Still was also active as a composer. In this role, he can proudly claim many "firsts." He was the first African American to conduct a major symphony orchestra in the United States, (Los Angeles Philharmonic Orchestra, 1936), the first to conduct a major symphony orchestra in the Deep South (New Orleans Symphony Orchestra, 1955), and the first to have an opera produced by a major company in the United States.

Answer Key

Page 5
1. presto
2. fermata
3. accent
4. andante
5. moderato
6. allegro
7. forte
8. dynamics
9. melody
10. phrase
Bonus: Handel

Page 6
Classic Rock: 4
The Beatles
Jimi Hendrix
Led Zeppelin
Janis Joplin

Jazz: 3
Miles Davis
Wynton Marsalis
Dizzy Gillespie

Pop Music: 3
Kelly Clarkson
Destiny's Child
Gwen Stefani

Country: 3
Johnny Cash
Patsy Cline
Faith Hill

Page 7
1. A
2. G
3. F
4. E
5. H
6. B
7. D
8. J
9. I
10. C

Page 8
1. speech
2. notable
3. delivered
4. blacks
5. named
6. address
7. children

Page 9

M	O	Z	T	R	T
Z	A	R	A	M	O
R	T	M	O	Z	A
O	M	T	R	A	Z
A	R	O	Z	T	M
T	Z	A	M	O	R

T	A	O	R	M	Z
R	Z	M	A	T	O
O	T	Z	M	A	R
A	M	R	O	Z	T
Z	O	A	T	R	M
M	R	T	Z	O	A

Page 10

Page 11
A. 4/4
B. 3/4
C. 4/4
D. 2/4
E. 6/8
F. 4/4
G. 4/4
H. 3/4
I. 6/8
J. 2/4
K. 4/4
L. 3/4

Page 12
1. Baroque
2. Religious
3. Germany
4. Opera
5. Messiah
6. Westminster Abbey
7. England

Page 14
Begin in the lower right-hand corner and go left.

Page 15
NOTE

Page 16
Chopin

Page 17
1. William Grant Still
2. Amy Beach
3. Handel

Page 18

L	N	A	D	E	H
D	A	H	E	L	N
E	H	N	L	D	A
N	D	E	A	H	L
A	E	L	H	N	D
H	L	D	N	A	E

N	A	H	L	E	D
L	E	N	D	H	A
D	H	E	A	L	N
H	D	L	N	A	E
E	N	A	H	D	L
A	L	D	E	N	H

Page 19
1. False
2. True
3. False
4. True
5. True
6. False
7. True
8. False
9. True
10. False
11. False
12. True
13. True
14. False
15. False

Answer Key

Page 20
1. Blue
2. Space
3. Breeze
4. Deep
5. Diameter
6. Chemical

Page 21
From L-R
fortissimo (upside down)
treble clef
bass clef (upside down)
fermata
eighth note
natural
flat
quarter rest (upside down)

Page 22
1. Beatle attended the wedding
2. good morning to all
3. comic book artist
4. jumping flea
5. melba toast
6. pig's squeal

Page 23
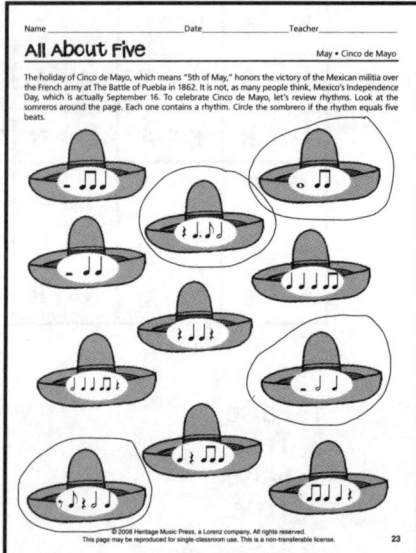

Page 24
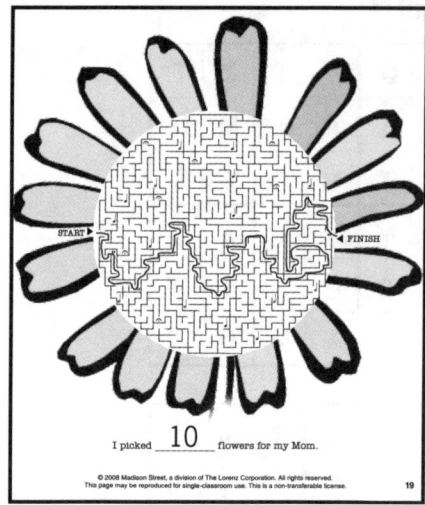

Page 25
Marching Band

Page 26
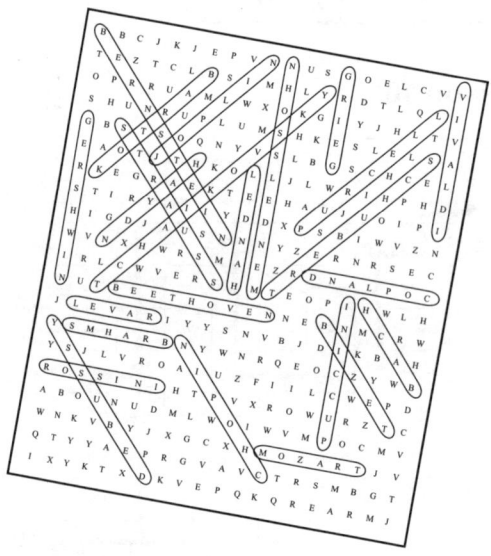

Page 28
Tuba = L
Snare Drum = H
Clarinet = H
Bells = H
Flute = H
Tambourine = H
Cabasas = H
Cello = L
Trombone = L
Harmonica = H
Horn = L

Page 29
Harmonica
Trumpet
Guitar
Triangle
Drum
Tambourine
Trombone

Page 30
Viola = yellow
Trumpet = blue
Tambourine = red
Oboe = green
Saxophone = green
Guitar = yellow
Tuba = blue
Flute = green
Timpani = red
Trombone = blue
Cello = yellow

Page 31
Harp = string
Mandolin = string
Cello = string
Saxophone = woodwind
Bassoon = woodwind
Flute = woodwind
Trumpet = brass
Timpani = percussion
Tambourine = percussion
Clarinet = woodwind
Violin = string
Marimba = percussion
Trombone = brass
Snare Drum = percussion
Cornet = brass

Page 32
Magic Flute

Page 33
Clarinet
Trombone
Snare Drum
Trumpet
Flute
Saxophone

Answer Key

Page 34

S	T	A	U	G	V
U	G	V	T	A	S
G	A	S	V	T	U
V	U	T	A	S	G
T	S	U	G	V	A
A	V	G	S	U	T

M	H	E	A	L	R
A	L	R	H	M	E
L	R	H	M	E	A
E	A	M	R	H	L
H	E	A	L	R	M
R	M	L	E	A	H

Page 35
L-R from top
3 scoops
3 scoops
1 scoop
4 scoops
4 scoops
2 scoops
1 scoop

Page 36
1. cornet
2. woodblocks
3. chordophone
4. electrophones

Page 37
1. chamber pot
2. sight; blind
3. Clara
4. The Red Priest
5. clavichord
6. sonatas; symphony
7. thirteen
8. macaroni; cheese

Page 38
1. broadway
2. classical
3. baroque
4. blues
5. rap
6. Latin
7. swing
8. romantic
9. rock
10. folk
11. hiphop
12. country
13. reggae

Bacon and Toast

Page 40
Start in lower left-hand corner and go up

Page 42
Bach = 4
- I was the master of the Baroque style.
- I spent my career working for royalty and the church.
- I wrote over 220 cantatas.
- I composed *The Well-Tempered Clavier*

Beethoven = 6
- I composed *Eroica*.
- I was one of Haydn's pupils.
- I was born in Bonn, Germany in 1770.
- I was recognized as the greatest living composer.
- By 1816, I was totally deaf.
- I was in demand as a teacher to children of royalty.

Mozart = 5
- I was born in Salzburg, Austria in 1756.
- I composed 21 operas.
- I was giving piano concerts for royalty by age seven.
- I lived to the age of 35.
- I composed an opera entitled *The Marriage of Figaro*.

Page 43
1. LABOR
2. CELEBRATION
3. BECAME
4. CLEVELAND
5. FALL
6. NEED

Page 44

1	Christina Aguilera	2	Meringue
4	Castanets	2	Palmas
2	Cumbia	1	Tito Puente
1	Placido Domingo	2	Rancheras
3	De Colores	2	Rhumba
3	El Jarabe Tapatío	2	Salsa
1	Manuel de Falla	2	Samba
2	Flamenco	1	Carlos Santana
3	Guantanamera	4	Spanish guitar
1	Antonio Carlos Jobim	4	Tambor
3	La Cucaracha	4	Vihuela
2	Mariachi		

Page 44
Tuba Player:
- Sound coming from bell
- 1 leg vs. 2
- Stripe and no stripe on pant leg
- Rank on sleeve is different

Bass Drum:
- Image reversed
- one is black the other is gray
- white vs. gray brackets

Trumpet:
- white vs. gray
- 3 valves vs. 2

63

answer key

Page 46
1. true
2. false
3. true
4. false
5. false
6. false
7. false
8. true
9. false
10. false
11. false
12. true
13. true
14. false
15. true

Page 47

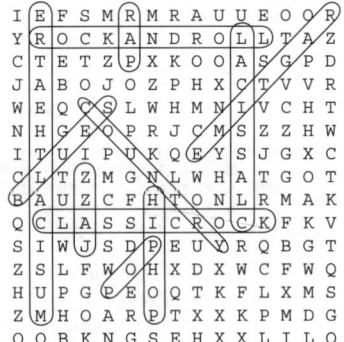

Page 48
1. medicine
2. composition
3. improvising
4. polyphony
5. choir
6. assignment
7. professional
8. revolutionary
9. theory
10. structured

Page 50

Page 51
Brass:
trumpet
flugelhorn
tuba

Woodwind:
piccolo
oboe
bassoon

String:
banjo
guitar
ukulele

Percussion:
claves
guiro
xylophone

Page 52
1. Purcell
2. guiro
3. flugelhorn
4. presto

Page 53
A. American Cheese, Turkey and Tomato

B. Roast Beef, Lettuce and Swiss Cheese

C. Tomato, Lettuce, Swiss Cheese and American Cheese

D. Roast Beef, Ham and Turkey

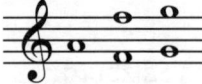

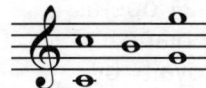

Page 54

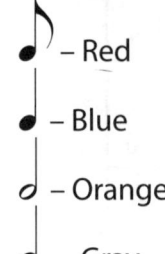 – Red

♩ – Blue

𝅗𝅥 – Orange

𝅗𝅥. – Gray

𝅝 – Purple

𝄽 – Pink

𝄽 – Light Blue

▬ – Yellow

▬ – Red Violet

Page 55
Moving L-R

1. Add 2 beats
2. Remove ½ a beat
3. Add 1 beat
4. Add 2 ½ beats
5. Add ½ a beat
6. Remove 3 beats
7. Add 3 beats
8. Remove 3 ½ beats
9. Add 2 ½ beats
10. Add 4 beats
11. This tray has 12 beats
12. Add 3 ½ beats

Page 57
1. conduct
2. accent
3. tempo
4. metronome
5. decrescendo
6. chord
7. slur
8. capo
9. natural
10. legato